Books and Plays in Films 1896–1915

Books by Denis Gifford

Space Patrol Handbook
Cinema Británico
British Cinema
Movie Monsters
Science Fiction Film
Discovering Comics
Stap Me! The British Newspaper Strip
Test Your Nostalgia Quotient
Fifty Years of Radio Comedy
A Pictorial History of Horror Films
The British Film Catalogue
Karloff the Man, the Monster, the Movies
Chaplin
Victorian Comics
The Armchair Odeon
Happy Days: 100 Years of Comics
The British Comic Catalogue
Run Adolf Run
The Best of Eagle
The Morecambe and Wise Comic Book
Monsters of the Movies
The Two Ronnies Comic Book
Stewpot's Fun Book
Eric and Ernie's TV Fun Book
Quick on the Draw
The Illustrated Who's Who in British Films
The Great Cartoon Stars
The British Comics and Story Paper Price Guide
The International Book of Comics
The Complete Catalogue of British Comics
The Golden Age of Radio
British Animated Films
The Encyclopedia of Comic Characters
Comics at War
The Eagle Book of Cutaways
The Story Paper Price Guide
The Comic Art of Charlie Chaplin
The Best of Eagle Annual
Bless 'Em All, the World War Two Song Book
The American Comic Book Catalogue
The Best of Girl Annual
American Animated Films

Books and Plays in Films 1896–1915

Literary, Theatrical and Artistic Sources of the First Twenty Years of Motion Pictures

Denis Gifford

McFARLAND

MANSELL

LONDON AND NEW YORK

First published 1991 by Mansell Publishing Limited
A Cassell imprint
Villiers House, 41/45 Strand, London WC2N 5JE, England
387 Park Avenue South, New York, NY 10016–8810, USA

Published in the United States of America by
McFarland & Company, Inc., Publishers
Box 611, Jefferson, North Carolina 28640, USA

British Library Cataloguing in Publication Data
Gifford, Denis *1927*-
Books and plays in films, 1896–1915: literary, theatrical and artistic sources of the first twenty years of motion pictures.
1. Books. Adaptations – Filmographies
I. Title
011.37

ISBN 0–7201–2080–2

Library of Congress Cataloging-in-Publication Data
Gifford, Denis.
Books and plays in films, 1896–1915 : literary, theatrical, and artistic sources of the first twenty years of motion pictures / by Denis Gifford.
p. cm.
Includes index
ISBN 0–89950–650–X (lib. bdg. : alk. paper)
1. Film adaptations—Catalogs. I. Title.
PN1997.85.G54 1991
016.79143'75--dc20 91–14174
CIP

Printed and bound in Great Britain by
Biddles Ltd, Guildford and King's Lynn

Contents

Introduction

This is the world's first catalogue of cinematograph films adapted from literary, artistic and other media sources for the period 1896 through 1915: the first twenty years of motion pictures. It includes novels, plays, non-fiction books, short stories, biographies, poems, operas, songs, cartoons and comic strips. The main arrangement is by author/creator, whose 861 names are arranged alphabetically, under which the film adaptations are listed chronologically. For each film title the first show date is given (month and year), the production company, the length, and an abbreviation giving a code to the type of source material. The film's title is given in full, together with any change of title by the film-makers from the author's original. Each entry is given an item number.

This book relates only to silent pictures, of course, and as production and distribution was global at the time, films are included from the United States of America, the United Kingdom, France, Germany, Italy, Australia, Canada, Scandinavia, Japan and other countries. A checklist of the 239 film companies included will be found as an appendix at the back of the book, arranged alphabetically by country.

There is an alphabetical index to film titles, with reference to the catalogue item numbers: a total of over 2,000 film and original source titles (where different). The actual total of films included in the catalogue would be closer to 3,000 as film titles are indexed only once, and many of the more popular or familiar titles were remade several times during our period.

When cinema began in 1896, films seldom ran to more than one minute (60 feet) in length. Even so it is surprising how many attempts were made to concentrate the meat of a popular novel or play into one flickering minute or two. Films soon grew in length and running time, from two minutes to five, ten, fifteen and twenty minutes, until by the close of our period, December 1915, the four- and five-reel feature film had become the mainstay of the average theatre programme.

Although very few of these primitive movies remain extant, even in the world of the national cinematheques, hopefully this book will give interested researchers and enthusiasts the opportunity to go back to the original sources and at least read the stories of what our ancestors were watching almost a century ago.

Any additions or corrections will be gratefully received by the author, in care of the publishers, and incorporated in any future editions of this catalogue.

Guide to Users

The authors/creators are listed alphabetically by surname, followed by given names. Where the name under which the work was first published is a pseudonym or pen-name, this is treated as the main name. Where known, the real name of the author is then given in parentheses. In addition, real names of authors appear in their alphabetical order, with cross-references to their pen-names. Where a work has more than one author, both authors are listed separately, with the note '*see also*' as a cross-reference; this includes adaptors and translators. Surnames beginning with 'de', 'le', 'von', etc. take various forms according to tradition or foreign practice. Cross references are therefore included where appropriate.

The films are listed chronologically in order of their first showing or release dates, giving both month (in abbreviated form) and year, where known. Where the release title of the film differs from the title of the original work, this original title is given in parentheses and in italics, below the film title. The production company of the film follows the title. The length of the film is given by a figure in parentheses. This indicates the number of reels to which the film ran: i.e. (1) is one reel, (2) is two reels, etc. The standard length of a reel of silent film was 1,000 feet. Where a film ran for less than a reel, the symbol (X) is used.

The final column of symbols indicates the type of literary or artistic source material upon which the film was based:

(B) ballet
(Bio) biography
(C) cartoon or comic strip
(Ch) character
(N) novel
(NF) non-fiction

(O) opera or operetta
(P) play or short theatrical sketch or skit
(Pm) poem
(S) short story
(Sg) song

Entries are presented according to the following format:

220[1] Doyle[2], Sir[3] Arthur Conan[4]

Dec[5] 1905[6] Sherlock Holmes Held to Ransom[7] *Urban*[8] (X)[9](N)[10]
(The Sign of the Four)[11]

1 Entry number
2 Surname
3 Title
4 Given names (plus real names, if a pseudonym)
5 Month of first showing/release
6 Year of first showing/release
7 Title of film
8 Production company
9 Length (in this case, less than one reel of 1,000 feet)
10 Source (in this case, a novel)
11 Original title of work upon which film is based

The Catalogue

1 ADAMS, A. H.

Sep 1909	The Evil That Men Do *('Ception Shoals)*	*Vitagraph*	(1)(S)

2 ADAMS, Frederic Justin

Dec 1912	Quincy Adams Sawyer *(see also* Pidgin)	*Puritan*	(1)(P)

3 ADE, George

Jun 1914	The Fable of the Brash Drummer and the Nectarine	*Essanay*	(1)(S)
Jun 1914	The Fable of the Good Fairy	*Essanay*	(1)(S)
Jul 1914	The Fable of Napoleon and the Bumps	*Essanay*	(1)(S)
Jul 1914	The Fable of the Higher Education That Was Too High for the Old Man	*Essanay*	(1)(S)
Jul 1914	The Fable of the Coming Champion Who Was Delayed	*Essanay*	(1)(S)
Aug 1914	The Fable of the Busy Business Boy and the Droppers-In	*Essanay*	(1)(S)
Aug 1914	The Fable of the Maneuvers of Joel and Father's Second Time on Earth	*Essanay*	(1)(S)
Aug 1914	The Fable of the Two Mandolin Players and the Willing Performer	*Essanay*	(1)(S)
Aug 1914	The Fable of the Difference between Learning and Learning How	*Essanay*	(1)(S)
Sep 1914	The Fable of the Regular Beanery and the Peachy Newcomer	*Essanay*	(1)(S)
Sep 1914	The Fable of the Honeymoon That Tried to Come Back	*Essanay*	(1)(S)
Sep 1914	The County Chairman	*Famous Players*	(4)(P)
Sep 1914	The Fable of Lutie the False Alarm	*Essanay*	(1)(S)
Sep 1914	The Fable of the One Samaritan Who Got Paralysis of the Helping Hand	*Essanay*	(1)(S)
Sep 1914	The Fable of the Adult Girl Who Got Busy	*Essanay*	(1)(S)
Oct 1914	The Fable of the Family That Made Too		

	Much of Nellie	*Essanay*	(1)(S)
Oct 1914	The Fable of the Author and the Dear Public and the Plate of Mush	*Essanay*	(1)(S)
Oct 1914	The Fable of the Long Range Lover and the Lollypalooze	*Essanay*	(1)(S)
Oct 1914	The Fable of the People's Choice Who Answered the Call of Duty and Took Seltzer	*Essanay*	(1)(S)
Oct 1914	The Fable of How Uncle Brewster Was Too Shifty for the Tempter	*Essanay*	(1)(S)
Nov 1914	Three Boiled down Fables	*Essanay*	(1)(S)
Nov 1914	The Fable Proving That Spongers Are Found in a Drugstore	*Essanay*	(1)(S)
Nov 1914	The Fable of Aggie and the Aggravated Attacks	*Essanay*	(1)(S)
Nov 1914	The Fable of the Club Girls and the Four Times Veteran	*Essanay*	(1)(S)
Dec 1914	The Fable of the Burlesque Lover Who Failed to Qualify	*Essanay*	(1)(S)
Dec 1914	Two Pop-up Fables	*Essanay*	(1)(S)
Dec 1914	The Fable of the Husband Who Showed up and Did His Duty	*Essanay*	(1)(S)
Dec 1914	Two Dinky Little Dramas of a Non-serious Kind	*Essanay*	(1)(S)
Dec 1914	The Slim Princess	*Essanay*	(4)(P)
Jan 1915	The Fable of the City Grafter and the Unprotected Rubes	*Essanay*	(1)(S)
Jan 1915	The Fable of the Fellow Who Had a Friend Who Knew a Girl Who Had a Friend	*Essanay*	(1)(S)
Jan 1915	The Fable of Hi-Faluting Tillie and Her Plain Parents	*Essanay*	(1)(S)
Jan 1915	The Fable of the Syndicate Lover	*Essanay*	(1)(S)
Jan 1915	The Fable of Elvira and Farina and the Meal Ticket	*Essanay*	(1)(S)
Feb 1915	The Fable of the Good People Who Rallied to the Support of the Church	*Essanay*	(1)(S)
Feb 1915	The Fable of the Cold Gray Dawn of the Morning After	*Essanay*	(1)(S)

Feb 1915	The Fable of the Bachelor and the Back Pedal	*Essanay*	(1)(S)
Feb 1915	A Couple of Side Order Fables	*Essanay*	(1)(S)
Mar 1915	The Fable of the Divine Spark That Had a Short Circuit	*Essanay*	(1)(S)
Mar 1915	The Fable of the Galumptious Girl	*Essanay*	(1)(S)
Mar 1915	The Fable of the Struggle Between Personal Liberty and the Wave of Reform	*Essanay*	(1)(S)
Mar 1915	The Fable of the Demand That Must Be Supplied	*Essanay*	(1)(S)
Mar 1915	The Fable of the Busy Man and the Idle Woman	*Essanay*	(1)(S)
Apr 1915	The Fable of the Men at the Women's Club	*Essanay*	(1)(S)
Apr 1915	The Fable of the Two Unfettered Birds	*Essanay*	(1)(S)
Apr 1915	The Fable of a Night Given Over to Revelry	*Essanay*	(1)(S)
Apr 1915	The Fable of the Galloping Pilgrim Who Kept on Galloping	*Essanay*	(1)(S)
May 1915	The College Widow	*Lubin*	(4)(P)
May 1915	The Fable of the High Roller and the Buzzing Blondine	*Essanay*	(1)(S)
May 1915	The Fable of the Two Sensational Failures	*Essanay*	(1)(S)
May 1915	The Fable of the Intermittent Fusser	*Essanay*	(1)(S)
Jun 1915	The Fable of the Search for Climate	*Essanay*	(1)(S)
Jul 1915	The Fable of the Scoffer Who Fell Hard	*Essanay*	(1)(S)
Jul 1915	Marse Covington	*Rolfe*	(5)(P)
Jul 1915	Betty's Dream Hero (*see also* Cochrane)	*Universal*	(2)(S)
Jul 1915	The Fable of the Home Treatment and the Sure Cure	*Essanay*	(1)(S)
Jul 1915	The Fable of the Tip and the Treasure	*Essanay*	(1)(S)
Aug 1915	Just Out of College	*Frohman*	(5)(P)
Aug 1915	The Fable of the Roistering Blades	*Essanay*	(1)(S)
Aug 1915	The Fable of Hazel's Two Husbands and What Became of Them	*Essanay*	(1)(S)
Sep 1915	The Fable of the Through Train	*Essanay*	(1)(S)
Sep 1915	The Fable of the Statesman Who Didn't Make Good	*Essanay*	(1)(S)
Oct 1915	The Fable of the Sorrows of the Unemployed and the Danger of		

	Changing from Bill to Harold	*Essanay*	(1)(S)
Oct 1915	The Fable of the Escape of Arthur and the Salvation of Herbert	*Essanay*	(1)(S)
Oct 1915	The Fable of the Handsome Jethro Who Was Simply Cut Out to Be a Merchant	*Essanay*	(1)(S)
Nov 1915	The Fable of the Lowdown Expert on the Subject of Babies	*Essanay*	(1)(S)
Dec 1915	Father and the Boys	*Universal*	(5)(P)
Dec 1915	The Fable of Sister Mae Who Did As Well As Could Be Expected	*Essanay*	(1)(S)
Dec 1915	The Fable of the Heir and the Heiress	*Essanay*	(1)(S)
Dec 1915	The Fable of the Two Philanthropic Sons	*Essanay*	(1)(S)

4 AESOP

May 1910	The Cat That Hated People	*Pathé*	(X)(S)

5 AINSWORTH, William Harrison

Mar 1909	The Tower of London	*Williamson*	(1)(N)
Sep 1913	King Charles *(Ovingdean Grange)*	*Clarendon*	(4)(N)
Jan 1914	Old Saint Paul's	*Clarendon*	(4)(N)

6 AISTON, Arthur C.

Aug 1914	At the Old Crossroads	*Select*	(5)(N)

7 ALDRICH, Thomas Bailey

Nov 1913	Judith of Bethulia	*Biograph*	(4)(Pm)

8 ALFRIEND, Edward M.

Mar 1914	The Great Diamond Robbery *(see also* Wheeler*)*	*Playgoers*	(5)(P)

9 ALLEN, Grant Blairfindie

Oct 1915	The Woman Who Did	*Broadwest*	(5)(N)

10 ANDERSEN, Hans Christian

Dec 1902	The Little Match Seller *(The Little Match Girl)*	*Williamson*	(X)(S)
Mar 1908	The Poor Little Match Girl *(The Little Match Girl)*	*Goodfellow*	(X)(S)
Dec 1908	Ib and Little Christina	*Clarendon*	(X)(S)
Sep 1910	The Little Match Seller's Christmas *(The Little Match Girl)*	*Éclipse*	(X)(S)
Dec 1913	Little Claus and Big Claus	*Dania*	(1)(S)
Dec 1914	The Little Match Girl	*Neptune*	(X)(S)

11 ANSTEY, F. (Thomas Anstey Guthrie)

Jan 1914	The Brass Bottle	*T & G*	(4)(N)

12 APPLIN, Arthur

Jun 1907	The Sons of Martha	*Warwick*	(X)(N)
Feb 1914	The Lure of London	*Barker*	(5)(N)
Apr 1915	The Sort of Girl Who Came from Heaven	*Vitagraph*	(1)(S)

13 ARBUCKLE, Macklyn

Nov 1915	The Reform Candidate	*Pallas*	(5)(N)

(see also Guest*)*

14 ARCHER, Edwin

Oct 1915	Divorced	*Triumph*	(5)(P)

15 ARDEN, Edwin

Feb 1914	Reconciled in Blood	*Selig*	(1)(S)
Nov 1914	The Eagle's Nest	*Lubin*	(5)(N)

(see also Smith, Arden R.*)*

16 ARISTOPHANES

Jan 1910	Lysistrata	*Gaumont*	(1)(P)

17 ARMSTRONG, Paul

Jun 1914	The Escape	*Reliance*	(7)(P)
Jun 1914	The Greyhound (*see also* Mizner)	*Life Photo*	(5)(P)
Jul 1914	Salomy Jane (*see also* Harte)	*California*	(5)(P)
Jan 1915	The Deep Purple (*see also* Mizner)	*Liebler*	(5)(P)
Feb 1915	Alias Jimmy Valentine	*Liebler*	(4)(P)
Sep 1915	The Lure of Woman (*The Renegade*)	*World*	(5)(P)
Oct 1915	Blue Grass	*Equitable*	(5)(P)
Oct 1915	The Bludgeon	*Equitable*	(5)(P)
Oct 1915	Via Wireless (*see also* Smith, Winchell)	*Pathé*	(5)(P)

18 ARTHUR, Joseph

Apr 1914	The Cherry Pickers	*Selig*	(2)(S)

19 ARTHUR, Timothy Shay (*see also* Pratt)

May 1903	Ten Nights in a Barroom	*Biograph*	(X)(N)
Oct 1903	Ten Nights in a Barroom	*Lubin*	(X)(N)
Jun 1909	Ten Nights in a Barroom	*Essanay*	(1)(N)
Oct 1910	Ten Nights in a Barroom	*Thanhouser*	(1)(N)
Jun 1911	Ten Nights in a Barroom	*Selig*	(1)(N)
Nov 1913	Ten Nights in a Barroom	*Photo Drama*	(5)(N)

20 ASKEW, Claude and Alice

Jul 1915	The Shulamite (*see also Knoblauch*)	*London*	(5)(N)

21 AUBER, Daniel (*see also* Scribe)

Dec 1907	Fra Diavolo	*Walturdaw*	(X)(O)
Dec 1908	Fra Diavolo	*SCAGL*	(1)(O)
May 1910	Fra Diavolo	*Pathé*	(1)(O)
May 1912	Fra Diavolo	*Solax*	(2)(O)
Jun 1912	Fra Diavolo	*Thanhouser*	(1)(O)

22 AUSTIN, May

Jul 1914	The King's Romance (*see also* Edmonds)	*B & C*	(3)(N)

23 AYRES, Ruby Mildred

Jul 1915	Somewhere in France (*None But the Brave*)	*Regal*	(3)(N)

24 BAILY, Waldron

Oct 1915	The Heart of the Blue Ridge	*Shubert*	(5)(N)

25 BAKER, Robert Melville

Dec 1914	The Conspiracy (*see also* Emerson)	*Famous Players*	(4)(P)

26 BALCH, Frederick Homer

Oct 1914	The Bridge of the Gods	*Keedrick*	(4)(N)

27 BALESTIER, Elliott

Aug 1915	Under the Fiddler's Elm	*Lubin*	(2)(S)

28 BALFE, Michael William

Apr 1909	The Bohemian Girl	*Pathé*	(X)(O)

29 BALMER, Edwin

Dec 1913	The Wolf of the City	*Selig*	(2)(S)
Feb 1914	At the Eleventh Hour	*Selig*	(2)(S)
May 1914	The Girl at His Side	*Lubin*	(2)(S)
Jan 1915	Attorney for the Defense	*Lubin*	(3)(S)

BALZAC *see* de Balzac

30 BANCROFT, George Pleydell

Mar 1911	Princess Clementina	*Barker*	(1)(S)
	(*see also* Mason, Alfred Edward Woodley)		

31 BARBOUR, Edwin

Aug 1914	Northern Lights	*Life Photo*	(5)(P)
	(*see also* Harkins)		

32 BARCLAY, Florence

Jun 1915	The Rosary	*Selig*	(5)(N)
	(*see also* Rose)		

BARNARD, Lady Anne *see* Lindsay

33 BARR, Robert

Dec 1914	The Premature Compromise	*Edison*	(2)(S)
Jan 1915	An Invitation and an Attack	*Edison*	(2)(S)

34 BARRETT, Wilson (William Henry Barrett)

Sep 1902	Fight with Sledgehammers (*The Sledgehammer*)	*Harrison*	(X)(P)
Oct 1904	The Sign of the Cross	*Haggar*	(X)(P)
Aug 1909	The Way of the Cross (*The Sign of the Cross*)	*Vitagraph*	(1)(P)
Dec 1914	The Sign of the Cross	*Famous Players*	(5)(P)

35 BARRIE, Sir James Matthew

Oct 1912	The Little Minister	*Vitagraph*	(2)(N)
Aug 1913	Shipwrecked *(The Admirable Crichton)*	*Kalem*	(2)(P)
Aug 1914	The Man of Her Choice *(The Admirable Crichton)*	*Powers*	(1)(P)
Jan 1915	The Little Minister	*Neptune*	(4)(N)

36 BARROWS, Wayne Groves

Dec 1914	The Law of the Range	*Bison*	(3)(Pm)

37 BARTHOLOMAE, Phillip

Jun 1915	Little Miss Brown	*Brady*	(5)(P)
Dec 1915	Over Night	*Brady*	(5)(P)

38 BARTLETT, Frederick Orrin

Nov 1915	The Seventh Noon	*Mutual*	(5)(N)

39 BASKCOMB, A. W.

Nov 1913	The Staff Dinner	*Urban*	(X)(P)

40 BATAILLE, Henri

Oct 1914	The Naked Truth	*Kleine*	(4)(N)

41 BAUM, Lyman Frank

Feb 1910	The Wizard of Oz	*Selig*	(1)(N)
Mar 1910	Dorothy and the Scarecrow *(The Wizard of Oz)*	*Selig*	(1)(N)
May 1910	The Land of Oz	*Selig*	(1)(N)
Sep 1914	The Patchwork Girl of Oz	*Oz*	(5)(N)
Oct 1914	The Magic Cloak of Oz	*Oz*	(5)(N)

Dec 1914	The Last Egyptian	*Oz*	(5)(N)
Feb 1915	The New Wizard of Oz *(The Wizard of Oz)*	*Oz*	(5)(N)

42 BAYLEY, E.T.

Nov 1904	The Mistletoe Bough	*Clarendon*	(X)(Pm)

43 BEACH, Rex Ellingwood

Dec 1909	Pardners	*Edison*	(1)(N)
Jan 1910	Out of the Night	*Edison*	(1)(S)
Feb 1910	With Bridges Burned	*Edison*	(1)(S)
May 1910	The Mule Driver and the Garrulous Mute	*Edison*	(1)(S)
Jun 1910	The Shyness of Shorty	*Edison*	(1)(S)
Nov 1910	Arms and the Woman	*Edison*	(1)(S)
Jan 1911	With Interest to Date	*Edison*	(1)(S)
Oct 1911	The Kid from the Klondike *(The Elusive Graft)*	*Edison*	(1)(S)
Mar 1912	The Mine on the Yukon *(The Thaw at Slisco's)*	*Edison*	(1)(S)
1913	The Barrier	*Broncho*	(N)
Jan 1913	The Vengeance of Durand	*Vitagraph*	(2)(S)
Apr 1914	The Spoilers	*Selig*	(9)(N)
Dec 1915	The Ne'er-do-well	*Selig*	(5)(N)

44 BEBAN, George

Aug 1915	An Alien *(The Sign of the Rose)*	*Ince*	(5)(P)

45 BEECHER, Robert Livingston

Dec 1914	The Best of the Year	*Reliance*	(2)(S)

46 BEERS, Ethelinda Elliott

Jul 1913	The Picket Guard	*Bison*	(2)(S)

47 BELASCO, David

Dec 1913	The Stranglers of Paris (*see also* Belot)	*Motion Drama*	(6)(P)
Feb 1914	The Squaw Man (*see also* Royle)	*Lasky*	(6)(P)
Apr 1914	The DuBarry	*Kleine*	(5)(P)
Sep 1914	La Belle Russe	*Regent*	(5)(P)
Nov 1914	Rose of the Rancho (*see also* Tully)	*Lasky*	(4)(P)
Jan 1915	The Girl of the Golden West	*Lasky*	(5)(P)
Jan 1915	The Girl I Left Behind Me (*see also* Files)	*Fox*	(5)(P)
Mar 1915	The Heart of Maryland	*Tiffany*	(5)(P)
Apr 1915	May Blossom	*Famous Players*	(5)(P)
May 1915	The Woman (*see also* De Mille, Henry Churchill; De Mille, William Churchill)	*Lasky*	(5)(P)
Oct 1915	Zaza (*see also* Berton)	*Famous Players*	(5)(P)
Oct 1915	Madame Butterfly (*see also* Long, John Luther)	*Famous Players*	(5)(P)

48 BELL, Robert Stanley Warren

Aug 1914	The Third God	*Climax*	(1)(S)

49 BELLINI, Vincenzo

Jun 1911	Norma	*Vesuvio*	(1)(0)

50 BELOT, Adolphe

Dec 1913	The Stranglers of Paris (*Les Étrangleurs*)(*see also* Belasco)	*Motion Drama*	(6)(N)

51 BENNETT, Arnold

Dec 1915	The Great Adventure (*Buried Alive*)	*Turner*	(5)(N)

52 BENNETT, Emerson

Oct 1912	Forest Rose	*Thanhouser*	(1)(N)

53 BENNETT-THOMPSON, Lillian

Jul 1914	The Seventh Prelude	*Essanay*	(2)(S)

54 BERGERE, Ouida

May 1915	The Esterbrook Case	*Vitagraph*	(5)(N)
Nov 1915	Saints and Sinners	*Vitagraph*	(5)(N)
Nov 1915	Wasted Lives	*Vitagraph*	(5)(N)

55 BERLYN, Alfred

Nov 1913	The Hand of a Child	*Clarendon*	(1)(Pm)
Nov 1913	Coming Home	*Clarendon*	(1)(Pm)

BERNARDIN de St Pierre *see* **De St Pierre**

56 BERNSTEIN, Henry

Apr 1910	The Thief *(Le Voleur)*	*Nordisk*	(1)(P)
Dec 1914	Samson	*Fox*	(5)(P)
Dec 1914	The Thief *(Le Voleur)*	*Fox*	(5)(P)
Jul 1915	Sold *(Le Secret)* *(see also* Erastov*)*	*Famous Players*	(5)(P)

57 BERTON, Pierre

Oct 1913	Zaza *(see also* Belasco*)*	*Famous Players*	(5)(P)

58 BERTRAM, Arthur (Arthur Pearson Ibbot)

Sep 1915 Esther Redeemed *Renaissance* (4)(N)
(The Wolf Wife)

59 BIZET, Georges Alexandre

Feb 1909 Torero Song *Lubin* (X)(O)
(Carmen)(see also Mérimée*)*

60 BLACHÉ, Herbert

Nov 1913 Shadows of a Great City *Hepworth* (4)(P)
(see also Hoffman*)*

61 BLACK, Ladbrooke

Feb 1915 A Cinema Girl's Romance *Samuelson* (4)(N)

62 BLACKMORE, Richard Doddridge

Jun 1911 Lorna Doone *Thanhouser* (1)(N)
Dec 1912 Lorna Doone *Clarendon* (3)(N)
Mar 1915 Lorna Doone *Biograph* (2)(N)

63 BLANEY, Charles E.

Oct 1914 Across the Pacific *Premier* (5)(N)
Oct 1915 The Little Church Around the Corner *Equitable* (5)(N)

BLASCO Ibáñez, Vicente *see* Ibáñez

64 BLIGHTON, Frank H.

Jan 1914 The Silent Death *Edison* (2)(S)
Nov 1914 The Tell-Tale Hand *Essanay* (3)(N)
Jan 1915 When Love and Honor Called *Essanay* (3)(N)

BLOCK, Rudolph *see* Lessing, Bruno

65 BLOSSOM, Henry

Oct 1913	Checkers	*All Star*	(6)(N)
	(*see also* La Shelle)		

BLYTH, Harry *see* Meredith, Hal

66 BOCCACCIO, Giovanni

Jun 1910	The Adventures of Boccaccio	*Pasquali*	(X)(Bio)
1912	The Decameron	*Vesuvio*	(4)(S)

67 BOLTWOOD, Edward

Jan 1915	A Farewell Dinner	*Majestic*	(2)(S)

68 BONELLI, William

Sep 1915	An American Gentleman	*Liberty*	(5)(N)

69 BOOTH, Edwin

Dec 1909	Richelieu	*Vitagraph*	(1)(P)
	(*see also* Lytton)		

70 BOOTHBY, Guy

Sep 1909	Dr Nikola	*Nordisk*	(1)(N)
Oct 1909	Dr Nikola in Tibet	*Nordisk*	(1)(S)
Nov 1909	Dr Nikola or the Hidden Treasure	*Nordisk*	(1)(S)

71 BOUCICAULT, Dion (Dionysius Lardner Boursiquot)

Jul 1903	The Octoroon	*Gaumont*	(X)(P)
Oct 1903	Murphy's Wake	*Gaumont*	(X)(P)
	(The Shaughraun)		
Jul 1906	Murphy's Wake	*Walturdaw*	(X)(P)
	(The Shaughraun)		

Aug 1907	The Shaughraun	*Vitagraph*	(X)(P)
Jan 1909	The Octoroon	*Kalem*	(1)(P)
Oct 1909	Onawanda	*Vitagraph*	(X)(P)
Aug 1911	The Colleen Bawn	*Yankee*	(1)(P)
Aug 1911	Kathleen Mavourneen	*Yankee*	(1)(P)
Oct 1911	The Colleen Bawn	*Kalem*	(1)(P)
Nov 1911	Arrah-Na-Pogue	*Kalem*	(1)(P)
Jan 1912	The O'Neill *(Erin's Isle)*	*Kalem*	(1)(P)
Dec 1912	The Shaughraun	*Kalem*	(3)(P)
Feb 1913	The Long Strike	*Imp*	(2)(P)
Feb 1913	Kathleen Mavourneen	*Imp*	(2)(P)
Mar 1913	Kathleen Mavourneen	*Edison*	(1)(P)
May 1913	London Assurance	*Reliance*	(3)(P)
Jul 1913	The Streets of New York	*Pilot*	(3)(P)
Nov 1913	The Octoroon	*Kalem*	(3)(P)
Jun 1914	Grimaldi	*Planet*	(1)(P)
Nov 1914	Rip Van Winkle (*see also* Irving; Storey)	*Vitagraph*	(2)(P)
Jul 1915	After Dark	*Brady*	(5)(P)
Dec 1915	After Dark	*Buckland*	(3)(P)

BOURSIQUOT, Dionysius Lardner *see* Boucicault, Dion

72 BOWER, Bertha Muzzy

Mar 1914	The Up-Hill Climb	*Selig*	(2)(S)
Jul 1914	When the Cook Fell Ill	*Selig*	(2)(S)
Jul 1914	The Reveler	*Selig*	(2)(S)
Aug 1914	Chip of the Flying U	*Selig*	(3)(N)
Sep 1914	The Lonesome Trail	*Selig*	(3)(S)
Sep 1915	How Weary Went Wooing	*Selig*	(2)(S)

73 BRADDON, Mary Elizabeth

Jul 1906	Lady Audley's Secret	*Walturdaw*	(X)(N)
Jul 1908	Lady Audley's Secret	*Kalem*	(X)(N)

May 1912	Lady Audley's Secret	*Imp*	(2)(N)
Oct 1912	Her Bitter Lesson *(Aurora Floyd)*	*Selig*	(1)(N)
Dec 1912	Aurora Floyd	*Thanhouser*	(2)(N)
Mar 1915	Aurora Floyd	*Biograph*	(2)(N)
Aug 1915	Lady Audley's Secret	*Fox*	(5)(N)

74 BRADLEY, Alice

Mar 1915	The Governor's Lady	*Lasky*	(5)(P)

75 BRADY, Cyrus Townsend

Feb 1914	Hearts Adrift	*Famous Players*	(5)(N)
May 1914	The Southerners	*Edison*	(3)(N)
May 1914	The Island of Regeneration	*Vitagraph*	(4)(N)
Jun 1914	The Ring and the Man	*Famous Players*	(4)(N)
Aug 1914	When the West Was Young	*Selig*	(2)(N)
Aug 1914	The Better Man	*Famous Players*	(5)(N)
Sep 1914	The Reparation	*Selig*	(2)(S)
Nov 1914	The Little Angel of Canyon Creek	*Vitagraph*	(5)(N)
Mar 1915	When Billings Was Late	*Selig*	(2)(S)
May 1915	A Child of God	*Reliance*	(4)(N)
May 1915	Their First Quarrel	*Vitagraph*	(5)(N)
Jun 1915	The Chalice of Courage	*Vitagraph*	(6)(N)
Jun 1915	Hearts and the Highway	*Vitagraph*	(5)(N)
Jul 1915	The Heights of Hazard	*Vitagraph*	(5)(N)
Jul 1915	The Island of Surprise	*Vitagraph*	(5)(N)
Aug 1915	West Wind	*Vitagraph*	(3)(N)
Nov 1915	Colton, U.S.N.	*Vitagraph*	(5)(N)
Dec 1915	Britton of the Seventh	*Vitagraph*	(5)(N)

BRAEME, Charlotte Mary *see* Clay, Bertha M.

76 BRENNAN, George Hugh

Nov 1915	The Luring Lights *(Anna Malleen)*	*Kalem*	(4)(N)

77 BRIDGES, Victor

Nov 1915	Mr Lyndon at Liberty	*London*	(5)(N)

78 BRIEUX, Eugène

1912	Blanchette	*Film d'Art*	(2)(P)
1912	The Red Robe *(La Robe Rouge)*	*Film d'Art*	(2)(P)
Oct 1915	Damaged Goods *(Les Avariés)*	*American*	(7)(P)

79 BRININSTOOL, Earl Alonzo

Oct 1913	The Ballyhoo's Story	*Vitagraph*	(1)(Pm)
Sep 1914	Silent Trails	*Vitagraph*	(1)(Pm)

80 BROADHURST, George Howells

Aug 1914	The Call of the North *(see also* White, Stewart Edward*)*	*Lasky*	(5)(P)
Sep 1914	The Dollar Mark	*Lasky*	(5)(P)
Oct 1914	The Man of the Hour	*Brady*	(5)(P)
Jan 1915	Wildfire	*Brady*	(5)(P)
Mar 1915	What Happened to Jones?	*Brady*	(5)(P)
Apr 1915	The Man Who Found Himself	*Brady*	(5)(P)
Jun 1915	The Price	*Cosmos*	(5)(P)

81 BRONTË, Charlotte

Apr 1910	Jane Eyre	*Cines*	(1)(N)
May 1910	Jane Eyre	*Thanhouser*	(1)(N)
Feb 1914	Jane Eyre	*Imp*	(2)(N)
Oct 1914	Jane Eyre	*Garrison*	(3)(N)
Aug 1915	Jane Eyre	*Biograph*	(3)(N)

82 BROOKS, Marion

Mar 1912	Heir Apparent	*Edison*	(1)(S)

May 1912	The Bank President's Son	*Edison*	(1)(S)
Jun 1912	The Passer-by	*Edison*	(1)(S)
Mar 1913	The Judge's Vindication	*Reliance*	(2)(S)
Apr 1913	The Half Orphans	*Majestic*	(2)(S)

83 BROWN, V.D.

Nov 1913	Jerry's Mother-in-Law (*see also* Lidell)	*Vitagraph*	(2)(S)

84 BROWNE, Porter Emerson

Jan 1915	A Fool There Was (*see also* Kipling)	*Fox*	(6)(P)
Jun 1915	The Spendthrift	*Kleine*	(5)(P)

85 BROWNE, Tom

Apr 1903	Weary Willie and Tired Tim: the Gunpowder Plot	*Warwick*	(X)(C)
Jul 1903	Weary Willie and Tired Tim Turn Barbers	*Warwick*	(X)(C)
Sep 1903	Weary Willie and Tired Tim: A Dead Shot	*Warwick*	(X)(C)
Feb 1904	Weary Willie in Search of Hidden Treasure	*Mitchell*	(X)(C)
Apr 1911	Weary Willie and Tired Tim: the Plum Pudding Stakes	*B & C*	(X)(C)
Apr 1911	Weary Willie and Tired Tim: the Sacred Elephant	*B & C*	(X)(C)
Apr 1911	Weary Willie and Tired Tim: Wanted, Field Marshals for the Gorgonzola Army	*B & C*	(X)(C)

Apr 1911	Weary Willie and Tired Tim: The Wild Wild Westers	*B & C*	(X)(C)

86 BROWNING, Elizabeth Barrett

Mar 1912	The Cry of the Children	*Thanhouser*	(2)(Pm)

87 BROWNING, Robert

Nov 1907	The Pied Piper of Hamelin	*Clarendon*	(X)(Pm)
Oct 1909	Pippa Passes	*Biograph*	(1)(Pm)
Feb 1910	The Pied Piper of Hamelin	*Edison*	(1)(Pm)
Jul 1911	The Pied Piper of Hamelin	*Thanhouser*	(1)(Pm)
Jan 1912	A Blot in the 'Scutcheon	*Biograph*	(1)(Pm)
Aug 1913	The Pied Piper of Hamelin	*Edison*	(1)(Pm)
Dec 1913	James Lee's Wife	*Rex*	(1)(Pm)
Apr 1914	Women and Roses	*Nestor*	(2)(Pm)
Sep 1914	The Light Woman	*Rex*	(2)(Pm)
Sep 1914	The Ring and the Book	*Biograph*	(3)(Pm)

88 BUCHANAN, Robert

Jan 1913	Fra Giacone	*Williams*	(1)(Pm)
Nov 1913	Phil Blood's Leap	*Clarendon*	(1)(Pm)
Mar 1915	The Trumpet Call (*see also* Sims)	*Neptune*	(4)(P)
Jun 1915	Alone in London (*see also* Jay)	*Turner*	(5)(P)

89 BUCHANAN, Thompson

Dec 1915	The Rack	*Brady*	(5)(N)

90 BUCK, Charles Neville

Oct 1914	The Key to Yesterday	*Favorite*	(4)(N)
Oct 1915	The Call of the Cumberlands	*Pallas*	(5)(N)

91 BUCKSTONE, John Baldwin

Nov 1912 Jack Sheppard *London* (3)(P)

92 BUNYAN, John

Oct 1912 The Pilgrim's Progress *Ambrosio* (4)(N)
1913 The Life of John Bunyan and 'The Pilgrim's Progress' *Hochstetter*(4)(Bio)

93 BURGESS, Frank Gelett

Jun 1914 The Persistent Mr Prince *Vitagraph* (1)(S)
Nov 1915 The Cave Man *Vitagraph* (5)(P)

94 BURNETT, Frances Hodgson

Jan 1914 A Lady of Quality *Famous Players* (5)(N)
Mar 1914 Little Lord Fauntleroy *Kinemalor* (5)(N)
May 1915 The Pretty Sister of José *Famous Players* (5)(N)
Jun 1915 The Dawn of a Tomorrow *Famous Players* (5)(N)
Sep 1915 Esmeralda *Famous Players* (5)(N)

95 BURNHAM, Clara Louise

Nov 1914 The Opened Shutters *Gold Seal* (4)(N)
Aug 1915 The Jewel *Universal* (4)(N)

96 BUSCH, Wilhelm

Apr 1907 Max und Moritz *L.K.* (X)(C)
Sep 1909 Papa's Honeymoon *(Max und Moritz)* *Lubin* (X)(C)
Jan 1912 Max and Maurice *(Max und Moritz)* *Edison* (1)(C)

97 BUTLER, Ellis Parker

Dec 1910 Pigs Is Pigs *Edison* (1)(S)

Jul 1914	Pigs Is Pigs	*Vitagraph*	(1)(S)
Dec 1914	Lena	*Edison*	(2)(S)
Jul 1915	The Shadow and the Shade	*Selig*	(1)(S)
Oct 1915	Hats Is Hats	*Vitagraph*	(1)(S)

98 BYRON, George Gordon, Lord

Feb 1908	Mazeppa	*Walturdaw*	(X)(Pm)
May 1908	Don Juan	*Pathé*	(1)(Pm)
1909	Mazeppa	*Thiemann*	(1)(Pm)
May 1910	Mazeppa	*Selig*	(1)(Pm)
Aug 1914	The Corsair	*Pathé*	(4)(Pm)

99 BYRON, Henry James

Mar 1915	Our Boys	*Kearton*	(3)(P)

100 BYRON, Oliver Doud

Oct 1913	Across the Continent	*Pilot*	(4)(N)

101 CAINE, Sir (Thomas Henry) Hall

Jun 1914	The Christian	*Vitagraph*	(8)(N)
Apr 1915	The Christian	*London*	(9)(N)
Apr 1915	The Eternal City	*Famous Players*	(5)(N)

102 CAMERON, George

Jul 1913	The Intruder	*Vitagraph*	(2)(S)
Jul 1913	The Late Mr Jones	*Vitagraph*	(2)(S)
Aug 1913	The Line-Up	*Vitagraph*	(2)(S)
Nov 1913	A Million Bid *(Agnes)*	*Vitagraph*	(5)(P)
Jan 1914	The Intruder	*Nestor*	(2)(S)
Dec 1915	Thou Art the Man	*Vitagraph*	(5)(P)

103 CAMP, Charles Wadsworth

Dec 1915	The Grey Mask	*Shubert*	(5)(N)

104 CAMPBELL, Bartlett Theodore

May 1913	The White Slave	*Vitagraph*	(2)(P)
Dec 1915	The Galley Slave	*Fox*	(5)(P)

105 CAMPBELL, Scott (Frederick Davis)

Oct 1914	The Case of the Vanished Bonds	*Edison*	(1)(S)
Nov 1914	Dickson's Diamonds	*Edison*	(1)(S)
Dec 1914	The Man Who Vanished	*Edison*	(1)(S)
Jan 1915	The Banker's Double	*Edison*	(1)(S)
Feb 1915	An Unpaid Ransom *(The Under Secretary)*	*Edison*	(1)(S)

106 CAREY, H. D.

Nov 1914	McVeagh of the Southern Seas	*Progressive*	(5)(N)

107 CAREY, Henry

Mar 1913	Sally In Our Alley	*Selig*	(1)(Pm)

108 CARLE, Richard (Charles Nicholas Carleton)

Nov 1915	Mary's Lamb	*Pathé*	(5)(P)

CARLETON, Charles Nicholas *see* Carle

109 CARLETON, William

Jun 1908	Over the Hill to the Poorhouse	*Biograph*	(1)(Pm)
Nov 1911	Over the Hills *(Over the Hill to the Poorhouse)*	*Imp*	(1)(Pm)
Jul 1912	Over the Hill to the Poorhouse	*Lubin*	(1)(Pm)
Dec 1912	The First Settler's Story *(Farm Festivals)*	*Edison*	(1)(Pm)

110 CARLILE, C. Douglas

Sep 1909	The Kidnapped King	*Gaumont*	(1)(P)

111 CARLTON, Henry Guy

Feb 1915	A Gilded Fool	*Box Office*	(4)(N)

112 CARPENTER, Edward Childs

Apr 1915	Captain Courtesy	*Bosworth*	(4)(N)
Dec 1915	The Tongues of Men	*Morosco*	(4)(P)

113 CARR, Catherine (Rosalind Herschel Wade)

Nov 1912	An Official Appointment	*Vitagraph*	(1)(S)
Feb 1914	In the Old Attic	*Vitagraph*	(1)(S)
Mar 1914	The Portrait	*Vitagraph*	(1)(S)
Apr 1915	Stage Money	*Vitagraph*	(2)(S)
Sep 1915	The Lesson of the Narrow Street	*Vitagraph*	(1)(S)
1915	Ward's Women	*Broncho*	(4)(N)

114 CARR, Comyns

Oct 1915	Called Back	*London*	(3)(P)

115 CARROLL, Lewis (Charles Lutwidge Dodgson)

May 1903	Alice in Wonderland *(Alice's Adventures in Wonderland)*	*Hepworth*	(1)(N)
Sep 1910	Alice's Adventures in Wonderland	*Edison*	(1)(N)
Jan 1915	Alice in Wonderland *(Alice's Adventures in Wonderland)*	*Nonpareil*	(4)(N)

116 CARTER, Daniel H. (David Daniel Cohen)

May 1914	The Master Mind	*Lasky*	(5)(P)

117 CARTER, Lincoln J.

Nov 1912	Chattanooga	*Carrowcliff*	(3)(P)
Mar 1913	Tbe Flaming Arrow	*Bison*	(2)(P)
Apr 1913	Bedford's Hope	*Bison*	(2)(P)
Apr 1913	The Indian's Secret	*Bison*	(2)(P)
Jun 1913	Two Little Waifs	*Bison*	(2)(P)
Jun 1913	The End of the Trail	*Bison*	(2)(P)

118 CARTER, Nick (John Russell Coryell)

Jul 1908	Nick Carter the King of Detectives and the Kidnappers' Plot	*Éclair*	(X)(S)
Aug 1908	The Great Jewel Affair	*Éclair*	(X)(S)
Sep 1908	The False Coiners	*Éclair*	(X)(S)
Sep 1908	The Bank Burglar	*Éclair*	(X)(S)
Dec 1908	Nick Carter in Danger	*Éclair*	(X)(S)
Jan 1909	Nick Carter's Double	*Pathé*	(X)(S)
Nov 1909	Nick Carter's Mysterious Luggage	*Éclair*	(X)(S)
Mar 1910	Nick Carter as Acrobat	*Éclair*	(X)(S)
1911	Zigomar vs Nick Carter	*Éclair*	(1)(S)
Apr 1912	Nick Carter	*Atlas*	(4)(N)

119 CARTON, R. C. (Richard Claude Crichett)

Dec 1914	Liberty Hall	*London*	(4)(P)
May 1915	Ashes of Revenge	*London*	(4)(N)

120 CASTLE, Agnes and Egerton

Dec 1914	The Incomparable Bellairs *(The Bath Comedy)*	*London*	(4)(N)
Aug 1915	The Secret Orchard *(see also* Pollock*)*	*Lasky*	(5)(N)

CERVANTES *see* de Cervantes

121 CHAMBERLAIN, Esther and Lucia

Aug 1913	The Coast of Chance	*Selig*	(1)(N)

Dec 1915	The Other Side *(The Other Side of the Door)*	*American*	(5)(N)

122 CHAMBERS, Charles Haddon

Feb 1914	The Idler	*Reliance*	(4)(P)
Oct 1914	Captain Swift	*Life Photo*	(5)(P)
Jan 1915	The Idler	*Box Office*	(5)(P)
Mar 1915	The Modern Magdalen	*Life Photo*	(5)(P)
Sep 1915	The Fatal Card *(see also* Stephenson*)*	*Famous Players*	(5)(P)

123 CHANFRAU, Frank S.

Sep 1914	The Arkansas Traveler	*Kalem*	(3)(S)

124 CHAPIN, Anna Alice

Jul 1914	The Eagle's Mate	*Famous Players*	(5)(N)
Dec 1914	The Under Trail	*Alliance*	(5)(N)

125 CHAPIN, Carl

Nov 1912	The Firefighter's Love *(The Test)*	*Selig*	(2)(S)

126 CHAPIN, Frederick

Dec 1914	The Sagebrush Girl	*Vitagraph*	(4)(N)
Dec 1914	C.O.D.	*Vitagraph*	(4)(N)
July 1915	The Revolt of Mr Wiggs	*Vitagraph*	(1)(S)

127 CHATEAUBRIAND, François Auguste René

Nov 1912	Atala	*Selig*	(1)(S)

128 CHATFIELD-TAYLOR, Hobart C.

Aug 1915	The Woman-Hater	*Essanay*	(3)(N)

Nov 1915	The Crimson Wing	*Essanay*	(6)(N)

129 CHATRIAN, Alexandre (*see also* Erckmann)

Feb 1913	The Bells *(Le Juif Polonais)*	*Reliance*	(2)(P)
Jun 1914	The Bells *(Le Juif Polonais)*	*Australia*	(4)(P)

130 CHESNEY, Arthur

Nov 1913	Daphne and the Dean	*Magnet*	(2)(P)

131 CHESTER, George Randolph

Feb 1913	The Cash Intrigue	*Utah*	(4)(N)
Dec 1913	The Manicure Girl	*Edison*	(1)(S)
Feb 1914	Back to Broadway	*Vitagraph*	(4)(N)
Mar 1914	The Girl from Prosperity	*Vitagraph*	(4)(N)
Jul 1914	Blue Peter's Escape	*Reliance*	(2)(N)
Jul 1914	Shadows of the Past	*Vitagraph*	(3)(N)
Sep 1914	The Making of Bobby Burnit *(see also* Smith, Winchell*)*	*Lasky*	(5)(N)
Dec 1914	The Man, the Mission and the Maid	*Vitagraph*	(4)(N)
Jan 1915	The Chief's Goat	*Vitagraph*	(4)(N)
Jan 1915	Runaway June *(see also* Chester, Lillian*)*	*Reliance*	(5)(N)
Oct 1915	The New Adventures of J. Rufus Wallingford	*Pathé*	(serial)(N)

132 CHESTER, Lillian

Jan 1915	Runaway June *(see also* Chester, George Randolph*)*	*Reliance*	(5)(N)

133 CHEVALIER, Albert

Aug 1911 My Old Dutch *Vitagraph* (1)(Sg)
Jun 1915 My Old Dutch *Turner* (5)(Sg)
(*see also* Shirley)

134 CHILD, Richard Washburn

May 1913 Her Big Story *American* (1)(S)
Jun 1914 The Man Who Disappeared *Edison* (1)(S)

135 CHURCHILL, Winston

Jan 1915 The Crisis *Selig* (12)(N)

136 CICCONI, Teobaldo

Sep 1914 A Great Mistake *Renowned* (6)(N)

137 CLANCY, Eugene

Jul 1914 A Tale of Old Tucson *Edison* (1)(S)

138 CLARETIE, Jules (Arsène-Arnaud)

Apr 1913 Little Jack *Pathé* (2)(N)
(Le Petit Jacques)

139 CLAUDY, Carl H.

Feb 1915 A Tragedy of the Rails *Edison* (2)(S)
(33 Runs Wild)

140 CLAY, Bertha M. (Charlotte Mary Braeme)

Aug 1910 Dora Thorne *Selig* (1)(N)
May 1912 Dora Thorne *Mutual* (2)(N)
Oct 1915 Dora Thorne *Biograph* (4)(N)
Oct 1915 His Wife *Thanhouser* (2)(N)
(My Poor Wife)

CLEMENS, Samuel Langhorne *see* Twain

141 CLERGET, Paul

Aug 1896	Two A.M., or The Husband's Return	*Paul*	(X)(P)

142 COCHRAN, R. H.

Mar 1915	The Arrival of Perpetua	*Shubert*	(5)(P)

143 COCHRANE, DeWitt

Jul 1915	Betty's Dream Hero *(see also* Ade*)*	*Universal*	(2)(S)

144 COGHLAN, Charles

Apr 1914	The Royal Box *(Kean)*	*Selig*	(2)(P)

COHEN, David Daniel *see* **Carter, Daniel H.**

145 COHEN, Octavus Roy

Jun 1915	The Honeymoon Baby	*Vitagraph*	(4)(S)

146 COLLINS, (William) Wilkie

Jun 1909	The Moonstone	*Selig*	(1)(N)
Nov 1910	The New Magdalen	*Powers*	(1)(N)
Oct 1912	The Woman in White	*Gem*	(2)(N)
Oct 1912	The Woman in White	*Thanhouser*	(2)(N)
Dec 1912	The New Magdalen	*Imp*	(2)(N)
May 1913	The Dead Secret	*Monopol*	(2)(N)
May 1913	Mercy Merrick *(The New Magdalen)*	*Edison*	(1)(N)
Feb 1914	The Dream Woman *(includes The Woman in White)*	*Blaché*	(5)(N)

Nov 1914	The New Magdalen	*Biograph*	(2)(N)
Jun 1915	The Moonstone	*World*	(5)(N)

147 COMFORT, William Levington

Dec 1913	The Glowworm	*Reliance*	(3)(S)
Jul 1914	The Sheriff of Contention *(The Angel of Contention)*	*Majestic*	(2)(S)

148 COMSTOCK, Harriet Theresa

Aug 1913	Joyce of the North Woods	*Edison*	(2)(S)
Oct 1913	Janet of the Dunes	*Edison*	(2)(S)
Jan 1914	Molly the Drummer Boy	*Edison*	(2)(S)

CONAN DOYLE *see* Doyle

149 CONNOR, Marie

May 1909	Convict 99 *(see also* Leighton*)*	*Gaumont*	(1)(N)

150 CONWAY, Hugh (Frederick Fargus)

Jun 1912	Called Back	*Thanhouser*	(2)(N)
Oct 1914	Called Back	*London*	(4)(N)
Nov 1914	Called Back	*Gold Seal*	(4)(N)

151 COOK, Edward

Mar 1915	Florence Nightingale *(The Life of Florence Nightingale)*	*B & C*	(4)(Bio)

152 COOKE, Baldwin G.

Oct 1914	His Last Dollar *(see also* Higgins*)*	*Famous Players*	(4)(S)

153 COOPER, Courtney Ryley

Nov 1913	The Ancient Order of Good Fellows	*Vitagraph*	(1)(S)
Aug 1914	Steve O'Grady's Chance	*Vitagraph*	(1)(S)
Aug 1914	One Touch of Nature	*Edison*	(1)(S)
Nov 1914	The Rocky Road of Love	*Vitagraph*	(2)(S)

154 COOPER, James Fenimore

Sep 1909	Leatherstocking	*Biograph*	(1)(N)
Jul 1911	The Last of the Mohicans	*Powers*	(1)(N)
Oct 1911	The Last of the Mohicans	*Thanhouser*	(1)(N)
Dec 1911	In the Days of the Six Nations *(The Last of the Mohicans)*	*Republic*	(2)(N)
Apr 1913	The Deerslayer	*Vitagraph*	(2)(N)
Jun 1913	The Pathfinder	*New York*	(2)(N)
Jun 1914	The Spy	*Universal*	(4)(N)

155 COPPÉE, François

Jun 1909	The Violin Maker of Cremona *(Le Luthier de Crémone)*	*Biograph*	(1)(P)
Mar 1910	The Violin Maker Of Cremona *(Le Luthier de Crémone)*	*Film d'Art*	(1)(P)
1912	For the Crown *(Pour la Couronne)*	*Film d'Art*	(2)(P)

156 CORELLI, Marie (Mary Mackay)

Jun 1910	Thelma	*Thanhouser*	(1)(N)
Jan 1911	Thelma	*Selig*	(1)(N)
Aug 1912	Thelma	*Reliance*	(1)(N)
Oct 1913	Vendetta	*SCAGL*	(2)(N)
Jun 1914	Vendetta	*Eclipse*	(5)(N)
Jun 1915	Wormwood	*Fox*	(5)(N)

157 CORNEILLE, Pierre

Jan 1910	Triumphant Hero *(Le Cid)*	*Cines*	(1)(P)

CORY, Vivian *see* **Cross, Victoria**

CORYELL, John Russell *see* **Carter, Nick**

COURCELLE *see* **De Courcelle**

158 COURTELINE, Georges (Georges Moineaux)

Dec 1913	The Funny Regiment *(Les Gaîtés de l'Escadron)*	*Union*	(3)(P)

159 COWAN, Laurence

Feb 1914	The World, the Flesh and the Devil	*Kinemacolor*	(5)(P)

160 COWPER, William

Aug 1908	John Gilpin *(The Diverting History of John Gilpin)*	*Clarendon*	(X)(Pm)
Oct 1908	John Gilpin's Ride *(The Diverting History of John Gilpin)*	*Hepworth*	(X)(Pm)

161 CRAIK, Dinah Maria

Nov 1910	John Halifax: Gentleman	*Thanhouser*	(1)(N)
Jun 1915	John Halifax: Gentleman	*Samuelson*	(5)(N)

162 CRAWFORD, Francis Marion

Sep 1913	A Cigarette Maker's Romance	*Hepworth*	(4)(N)
Jun 1913	The White Sister	*Essanay*	(5)(N)
Oct 1915	In the Palace of the King	*Essanay*	(5)(N)

CRICHETT, Richard Claude *see* **Canton**

CROISSET *see* de Croisset

CROSS, Marian Evans *see* Eliot, George

163 CROSS, Victoria (Vivian Cory)

Oct 1914	Life's Shop Window	*Box Office*	(5)(N)
May 1915	Five Nights	*Barker*	(6)(N)
Nov 1915	Paula	*Holmfirth*	(6)(N)

164 CROTHERS, Rachel

Dec 1914	The Three of Us	*Rolfe*	(4)(P)

165 CRUIKSHANK, George

May 1915	The Bottle	*Hepworth*	(3)(C)

(see also Shirley*)*

166 CURTIS, Edward Sheriff

Feb 1915	In the Land of the Headhunters	*World*	(5)(N)

167 CURWOOD, James Oliver

Dec 1910	Looking Forward	*Thanhouser*	(1)(S)
May 1911	The Prejudice of Pierre Marie	*Vitagraph*	(1)(S)
Aug 1912	Phillip Steele	*Reliance*	(2)(S)
Jan 1913	Duty and the Man	*Reliance*	(2)(S)
Mar 1913	The Strength of Men	*Vitagraph*	(2)(S)
Apr 1913	A Fighting Chance	*Vitagraph*	(1)(S)
Apr 1913	Diamond Cut Diamond	*Lubin*	(1)(S)
Jun 1913	Does Advertising Pay?	*Vitagraph*	(1)(S)
Jul 1913	The Feudists	*Vitagraph*	(2)(S)
Jul 1913	Why Am I here?	*Vitagraph*	(1)(S)

Aug 1913	When Women Go on the Warpath	*Vitagraph*	(1)(S)
Sep 1913	Fortune's Turn	*Vitagraph*	(1)(S)
Sep 1913	The Lost Millionaire	*Vitagraph*	(2)(S)
Sep 1913	Four Minutes Late	*Selig*	(2)(S)
Sep 1913	The Mystery of the Silver Skull	*Vitagraph*	(2)(S)
Sep 1913	Wheels of Fate	*Selig*	(2)(N)
Sep 1913	The Treasure of Desert Isle	*Vitagraph*	(1)(S)
Oct 1913	The Pirates	*Vitagraph*	(2)(S)
Oct 1913	Betty in the Lion's Den	*Vitagraph*	(1)(S)
Nov 1913	The War Makers	*Vitagraph*	(2)(S)
Nov 1913	Their Wives' Indiscretion	*Essanay*	(1)(S)
Nov 1913	Thor, Lord of the Jungles	*Selig*	(3)(N)
Nov 1913	Venus and Adonis	*Selig*	(2)(S)
Nov 1913	Memories That Hurt	*Vitagraph*	(2)(S)
Apr 1914	A Midnight Call	*Selig*	(1)(S)
Apr 1914	A Flirt's Repentance	*Selig*	(1)(S)
May 1914	Children of Fate	*Nestor*	(2)(S)
May 1914	Second Childhood	*Selig*	(1)(S)
Jun 1914	Wilderness Mail	*Selig*	(2)(N)
Jun 1914	Hearts of Men	*Selig*	(2)(S)
Jun 1914	His Fight	*Selig*	(1)(S)
Jun 1914	In Defiance of the Law *(The Trail's End)*	*Selig*	(3)(N)
Jun 1914	Caryl of the Mountains	*Selig*	(1)(S)
Jul 1914	His Flight	*Selig*	(1)(S)
Jul 1914	The Skull and the Crown	*Selig*	(2)(S)
Aug 1914	The White Mouse	*Selig*	(2)(S)
Aug 1914	The Speck on the Wall	*Selig*	(2)(S)
Aug 1914	Polishing Up	*Vitagraph*	(2)(S)
Aug 1914	The Ordeal	*Selig*	(2)(S)
Sep 1914	The Eugenic Girl	*Selig*	(1)(S)
Sep 1914	Ye Vengeful Vagabonds	*Selig*	(2)(S)
Sep 1914	The Fifth Man	*Selig*	(3)(N)
Oct 1914	Playing with Fire	*Selig*	(2)(S)
Oct 1914	His Dominant Passion	*Vitagraph*	(2)(S)
Oct 1914	The Man-Hater	*Selig*	(2)(S)
Oct 1914	The Dream Girl	*Selig*	(2)(S)
Nov 1914	The Mystery of the Seven Chests	*Selig*	(2)(S)

Nov 1914	The Tragedy That Lived	*Selig*	(2)(S)
Nov 1914	Two Women	*Vitagraph*	(3)(S)
Nov 1914	The Story of the Blood-red Rose	*Selig*	(3)(S)
Nov 1914	The Fatal Note	*Selig*	(2)(S)
Dec 1914	The Strange Case of Princess Kahn	*Selig*	(2)(S)
Dec 1914	Till Death Us Do Part	*Selig*	(2)(S)
Dec 1914	The Test	*Selig*	(2)(S)
Jan 1915	His Fighting Blood	*Selig*	(2)(S)
Jan 1915	The Spirit of the Violin	*Selig*	(2)(S)
Jan 1915	The Old Code	*Selig*	(2)(S)
Jan 1915	The Richest Girl in the World	*Selig*	(2)(S)
Feb 1915	Cats	*Selig*	(1)(S)
Feb 1915	The Lady Killer	*Selig*	(1)(S)
Feb 1915	The Red Blood of Courage	*Selig*	(2)(S)
Feb 1915	The Young Man Who Figgered	*Vitagraph*	(2)(S)
Feb 1915	A Pound for a Pound	*Essanay*	(2)(S)
Mar 1915	Retribution	*Selig*	(2)(S)
Mar 1915	A Study in Tramps	*Vitagraph*	(1)(S)
Mar 1915	The Battle of Frenchman's Run	*Vitagraph*	(2)(S)
Apr 1915	Getting a Start in Life	*Selig*	(2)(S)
Apr 1915	The Great Experiment	*Selig*	(2)(S)
Apr 1915	The Poetic Justice of Omar Khan	*Selig*	(2)(S)
May 1915	In the Days of Famine	*Vitagraph*	(3)(S)
May 1915	The Awakening	*Vitagraph*	(2)(S)
Jun 1915	Beautiful Belinda	*Selig*	(2)(S)
Jun 1915	The Mystery of Dead Man's Isle	*Selig*	(2)(S)
Jul 1915	The Coyote	*Selig*	(2)(S)
Sep 1915	The Jungle Lovers	*Selig*	(3)(S)
Sep 1915	Man's Law	*Selig*	(2)(S)
Sep 1915	Rags and the Girl	*Vitagraph*	(1)(S)
Oct 1915	The Gods Redeem	*Vitagraph*	(2)(S)
Oct 1915	Queen of Jungle Land	*Bison*	(3)(N)
Oct 1915	The Vengeance of Rannah	*Selig*	(2)(S)
Nov 1915	The Flashlight	*Selig*	(2)(S)

168 DALY, Augustin (*see also* Von Mosenthal)

Oct 1908	Leah the Forsaken	*Vitagraph*	(1)(P)

Sep 1912	Leah the Forsaken	*Imp*	(1)(P)

169 DANBY, Frank (Julia Davis Frankau)

Jul 1915	The Heart of a Child	*London*	(4)(N)

170 D'ANNUNZIO, Gabriele

1910	Francesca Da Rimini	*SCAGL*	(1)(P)
Sep 1911	Jorio's Daughter *(The Daughter of Jorio)*	*Ambrosio*	(1)(P)
Dec 1911	The Blood Vengeance	*Ambrosio*	(1)(P)
Jan 1912	An Autumn Sunset Dream *(Dream of an Autumn Sunset)*	*Ambrosio*	(1)(Pm)
Feb 1913	Marcus the Venetian Tribune	*Ambrosio*	(2)(P)
Jun 1915	The Devil's Daughter *(La Gioconda)(see also* Trant*)*	*Fox*	(5)(P)

171 DANTE Alighieri

1909	The Inferno	*Milano*	(X)(Pm)
1910	Dante's Inferno	*Edison*	(1)(Pm)
1911	Dante's Inferno	*Monopol*	(1)(Pm)
Apr 1911	Dante's Inferno	*Milano*	(5)(Pm)
Oct 1911	Dante's Inferno	*Helios*	(2)(Pm)
Dec 1911	Purgatory and Paradise	*Helios*	(4)(Pm)
1912	Purgatorio	*Milano*	(Pm)
1912	Dante and Beatrice *(Paradiso)*	*Milano*	(Pm)

172 D'ARCY, Hugh Antoine

Jun 1908	The Face on the Barroom Floor	*Edison*	(X)(Pm)
Jul 1908	The Face on the Barroom Floor	*Lubin*	(X)(Pm)
Dec 1912	Madeleine's Christmas	*Lubin*	(1)(Pm)
Aug 1914	The Face on the Barroom Floor	*Keystone*	(1)(Pm)

173 DARE, Walter

Oct 1915	The Little Gypsy	*Fox*	(5)(N)

174 DARLINGTON, Charles

Aug 1914	Heart Beats *(A Useless Crime)*	*Ideal*	(3)(N)

175 DARNLEY, Herbert

Jul 1908	Napoleon and the English Sailor	*Gaumont*	(X)(P)
Jul 1908	Moving in	*Gaumont*	(X)(P)

176 DARRELL, Charles

Aug 1914	When London Sleeps	*B & C*	(3)(P)
Nov 1914	Her Luck in London	*B & C*	(4)(P)
Dec 1914	The Idol of Paris	*B & C*	(3)(P)
Mar 1915	From Shopgirl to Duchess	*B & C*	(4)(P)

177 DAUDET, Alphonse

Apr 1908	Sappho *(Sapho)*	*Essanay*	(1)(N)
Nov 1908	L'Arlésienne	*SCAGL*	(2)(P)
Aug 1912	Sappho	*Atlas*	(2)(N)
Jun 1913	Sappho	*Éclair*	(4)(N)
Sep 1913	Sappho	*Majestic*	(3)(N)
Dec 1913	Jack	*Éclair*	(4)(S)

178 DAVIS, Charles Belmont

Apr 1914	Countess Veschi's Jewels	*Vitagraph*	(4)(N)
Mar 1915	Countess Veschi's Jewels	*Essanay*	(4)(N)
Jun 1915	A Studio Escapade *(Escape)*	*Selig*	(S)
Jul 1915	The Octopus *(see also* Norris*)*	*Selig*	(3)(N)
Oct 1915	The White Light of Publicity	*Selig*	(4)(S)

179 DAVIS, Christopher

Dec 1912	The Fighting Parson (*see also* Gray, George)	*Barkar*	(2)(P)

DAVIS, Frederick *see* Campbell, Scott

180 DAVIS, Owen

Nov 1914	The Wishing Ring	*Shubert*	(5)(P)
Nov 1914	Lola	*Shubert*	(5)(P)
Dec 1914	The Marked Woman	*Peerless*	(5)(P)
Apr 1915	Hearts in Exile (*see also* Oxenham)	*Shubert*	(5)(P)
Aug 1915	The Woman Next Door	*Kleine*	(5)(P)
Oct 1915	The Family Cupboard	*Brady*	(5)(P)
Nov 1915	The Sentimental Lady	*Kleine*	(5)(P)
Nov 1915	The Green Cloak	*Kalem*	(5)(P)
Dec 1915	The Gambler of the West	*Biograph*	(5)(P)

181 DAVIS, Richard Harding

Mar 1910	Ranson's Folly	*Edison*	(1)(S)
Apr 1910	Her First Appearance	*Edison*	(1)(S)
Apr 1910	Gallegher	*Edison*	(1)(S)
Dec 1910	The Winning of Miss Langton (*Peace Maneuvers*)	*Edison*	(1)(P)
Dec 1910	The Romance of Hefty Burke (*Romance in the Life of Hefty Burke*)	*Edison*	(1)(S)
Jan 1911	An Eventful Evening (*Miss Civilization*)	*Edison*	(1)(P)
Mar 1911	The Disreputable Mr Reagan	*Edison*	(1)(S)
May 1911	How the Hungry Man Was Fed	*Edison*	(1)(S)
Aug 1911	Van Bibber's Experiment (*Van Bibber's Burglar*)	*Edison*	(1)(S)
Aug 1911	The Crucial Test (*The Derelict*)	*Edison*	(1)(S)
Dec 1911	How Sir Andrew Lost His Vote (*In the Fog*)	*Edison*	(1)(S)

Jan 1912	Eleanore Cuyler	*Edison*	(1)(S)
Jan 1914	Soldiers of Fortune *(see also* Thomas, Augustus*)*	*All Star*	(6)(N)
Nov 1914	The Man Who Could Not Lose	*Favorite*	(5)(S)
Dec 1914	The Last Chapter *(The Unfinished Story)*	*Favorite*	(5)(S)
Mar 1915	The Lost House	*Majestic*	(4)(S)
Apr 1915	Captain Macklin	*Majestic*	(4)(S)
Jun 1915	The Galloper	*Pathé*	(5)(P)
Jun 1915	The Dictator	*Famous Players*	(5)(P)
Sep 1915	Ranson's Folly	*Edison*	(5)(S)
Sep 1915	Playing Dead	*Vitagraph*	(5)(S)
Dec 1915	The Buried Treasure of Cobre	*Selig*	(5)(S)

182 DAZEY, Frank M.

1915	The Mating *(The Winning of Denise)*	*Domino*	(5)(N)

183 DE BALZAC, Honoré

Mar 1909	The Magic Parchment *(La Peau de Chagrin)*	*Pathé*	(X)(N)
Sep 1909	La Grande Breteche	*Pathé*	(1)(S)
Nov 1909	Ferragus	*Film d'Art*	(X)(N)
Dec 1909	La Duchesse de Langeais	*Pathé*	(1)(N)
Apr 1910	Eugénie Grandet	*Éclair*	(1)(N)
1910	Eugénie Grandet	*Film d'Art*	(1)(N)
1911	César Birotteau	*Éclair*	(1)(N)
1911	Le Colonel Chabert	*Pathé*	(1)(N)
1911	Le Peau de Chagrin	*SCAGL*	(1)(N)
Jan 1914	The Magic Skin *(La Peau de Chagrin)*	*Victor*	(2)(N)
Apr 1914	The Master Criminal *(La Fausse Maîtresse)*	*World*	(4)(N)

Dec 1914	Cousin Pons	*Biograph*	(4)(N)
Feb 1915	Père Goriot	*Biograph*	(2)(N)
Aug 1915	The Country Parson *(Le Curé de Village)*	*Biograph*	(4)(N)
Oct 1915	The Magic Skin *(La Peau de Chagrin)*	*Edison*	(5)(N)

184 DE BEAUMONT, Madame Le Prince

Jun 1908	Beauty and the Beast *(see also* Suzanne*)*	*Pathé*	(X)(S)

185 DE BRISAYS

Dec 1913	The Guerrillas of Algiers *(Jean de Poudre)*	*Ideal*	(S)

186 DE CAILLAVET, Gaston Arman

Dec 1912	The Merry Widow *(La Veuve Joyeuse)*	*Éclair*	(2)(O)

187 DE CERVANTES, Miguel

Dec 1904	The Adventures of Don Quixote	*Pathé*	(X)(N)
Jul 1908	Don Quixote's Dream	*Hepworth*	(X)(N)
Oct 1908	Incident from Don Quixote	*Méliès*	(X)(N)
Sep 1909	Don Quixote	*Gaumont*	(1)(N)
Mar 1911	Don Quixote	*Cines*	(1)(N)
Dec 1915	Don Quixote	*Fine Arts*	(5)(N)

188 DE COURCELLE, Pierre

Jul 1905	Two Little Vagabonds *(Les Deux Gosses)*	*Pathé*	(1)(P)

1914	Two Little Vagabonds *(Les Deux Gosses)*	*Pathé*	(4)(P)
1915	Plus Que Reine	*Pathé*	(5)(P)

189 DE CROISSET, François (Frantz Wiener)

Aug 1915	The Marriage of Kitty *(La Passerelle)(see also* De Gresac*)*	*Lasky*	(5)(P)

190 DEFOE, Daniel

1902	Robinson Crusoe	*Pathé*	(X)(N)
1903	Robinson Crusoe	*Méliès*	(1)(N)
Aug 1910	Robinson Crusoe	*Nordisk*	(1)(N)
May 1913	Robinson Crusoe	*Bison*	(3)(N)

191 DE GRESAC, Fred

May 1915	Cora	*Metro*	(5)(P)
Aug 1915	The Marriage of Kitty *(La Passerelle)(see also* De Croisset*)*	*Lasky*	(5)(P)

192 DEHAN, Richard (Clotilda Inez Mary Graves)

Nov 1915	The Dop Doctor	*Samuelson*	(6)(N)

193 DE JANVIER, F. H.

Feb 1914	The Sleeping Sentinel	*Lubin*	(1)(S)

DE LA FONTAINE *see* La Fontaine

194 DE LANA

Sep 1914	Poppies *(The Garden of Sleep)(see also* Scott, Clement William*)*	*Climax*	(1)(Pm)

195 DELANO, Edith Barnard

Jun 1915	Rags	*Famous Players*	(5)(N)
Aug 1915	The Heart of Jennifer	*Famous Players*	(5)(N)
Oct 1915	The White Pearl	*Famous Players*	(5)(N)
Dec 1915	Still Waters	*Famous Players*	(5)(N)

DE LA RAMÉE, Louise *see* Ouida

196 DELIBES, Léo

Feb 1910	The Toymaker's Secret *(Coppélia)*	*Vitagraph*	(1)(B)
1913	Coppélia	*Pathé*	(1)(B)

197 DE LORDE, André

May 1914	The Lunatics *(Dr Goudron's System)*	*Leading Players*	(2)(S)
1914	Bagnes d'Enfants	*Éclair*	(1)(S)

198 DE MAUPASSANT, Guy

Jul 1909	The Necklace *(A String of Pearls)*	*Biograph*	(X)(S)
Aug 1909	The Coward	*Edison*	(X)(S)
Feb 1910	A Voice from the Fireside	*Essanay*	(X)(S)
Jun 1911	The Piece of String	*Imp*	(1)(S)
Jul 1912	The Blind Man's Sacrifice	*Milano*	(1)(S)
Aug 1912	At the Eleventh Hour *(A String of Pearls)*	*Vitagraph*	(1)(S)
Aug 1912	Her Hour of Triumph *(A String of Pearls)*	*Essanay*	(1)(S)

199 DEMESSE, Henri

May 1913	The Crime on the Coast *(La Petite Fifi)*	*Film d'Art*	(2)(S)

1914	La Dame Blonde	*Éclair*	(2)(S)

200 DE MILLE, Cecil Blount

Jan 1915	After Five *(see also* De Mille, William Churchill*)*	*Lasky*	(5)(P)
Apr 1915	The Captive	*Lasky*	(5)(P)

201 DE MILLE, Henry Churchill

Jun 1914	Lord Chumley	*Biograph*	(4)(P)
Aug 1914	Men and Women	*Klaw & Erlanger*	(3)(P)
Sep 1914	The Lost Paradise *(see also* Fulda*)*	*Famous Players*	(5)(P)
May 1915	The Woman *(see also* Belasco; De Mille, William Churchill*)*	*Lasky*	(5)(P)

202 DE MILLE, William Churchill

May 1914	Classmates *(see also* Turnbull, Margaret*)*	*Klaw & Erlanger*	(3)(P)
Jun 1914	Strongheart	*Klaw & Erlanger*	(3)(P)
Jan 1915	Young Romance	*Lasky*	(5)(P)
Jan 1915	After Five *(see also* De Mille, Cecil Blount*)*	*Lasky*	(5)(P)
Feb 1915	The Warrens of Virginia	*Lasky*	(5)(P)
May 1915	The Woman *(see also* Belasco; De Mille, Henry Churchill*)*	*Lasky*	(5)(P)
May 1915	The Wild Goose Chase	*Lasky*	(5)(P)
Aug 1915	The Puppet Crown *(see also* MacGrath, Harold*)*	*Lasky*	(5)(P)

203 DE MUSSET, Alfred

Oct 1909	Love Should Not Be Trifled with *(On ne badine pas avec l'Amour)*	*Pathé*	(X)(P)

Feb 1910	Barberine *(La Quenouille de Barberine)*	*Éclair*	(1)(P)
Apr 1910	Simone	*Pathé*	(X)(S)

204 DE NAVARRO, Carlos

Apr 1914	Mareea the Half-breed	*Vitagraph*	(2)(S)
Oct 1914	Mareea the Foster Mother	*Vitagraph*	(2)(S)

205 DENISON, Webster

Jul 1915	The Reverend Salamander Unattached	*Essanay*	(1)(S)

206 D'ENNERY, Adolphe

Sep 1902	Duel Scene from The Two Orphans *(The Two Orphans)*	*Haggar*	(X)(P)
Aug 1907	The Two Orphans	*Pathé*	(X)(P)
1909	The Two Orphans	*SCAGL*	(2)(P)
Jan 1910	A Celebrated Case	*Phoenix*	(1)(P)
Oct 1911	The Two Orphans	*Selig*	(1)(P)
Sep 1912	A Celebrated Case	*Gem*	(2)(P)
1913	The Two Orphans	*Pathé*	(4)(P)
Feb 1914	A Celebrated Case	*Kalem*	(4)(P)
Jul 1915	Don César de Bazan	*Kalem*	(4)(P)
Sep 1915	The Two Orphans	*Fox*	(5)(P)

207 DENTON, Jack

Oct 1909	Sexton Blake *(Sexton Blake Detective) (see also* Graydon; Meredith, Hal*)*	*Gaumont*	(1)(P)

208 DE ST PIERRE, Jacques Henri Bernardin

1910	Paul and Virginia *(Paul et Virginie)*	*Thanhouser*	(1)(S)
Dec 1912	Paul and Virginia *(Paul et Virginie)*	*Rex*	(2)(S)

209 DICKENS, Charles

Aug 1898	Mr Bumble, the Beadle *(Oliver Twist)*	*Paul*	(X)(N)
Nov 1901	Scrooge, or Marley's Ghost *(A Christmas Carol)*	*Paul*	(X)(S)
Nov 1901	Mr Pickwick's Christmas at Wardle's *(The Pickwick Papers)*	*Paul*	(X)(S)
Nov 1903	Dotheboys Hall, or Nicholas Nickleby *(Nicholas Nickleby)*	*Gaumont*	(X)(N)
Nov 1904	Gabriel Grub, The Surly Sexton *(The Pickwick Papers)*	*Williamson*	(X)(N)
Dec 1905	Oliver Twist	*Gaumont*	(1)(N)
Mar 1906	The Modern Oliver Twist *(Oliver Twist)*	*Vitagraph*	(1)(N)
Nov 1908	A Christmas Carol	*Essanay*	(1)(S)
Jan 1909	The Old Curiosity Shop	*Essanay*	(1)(N)
Feb 1909	The Mystery of Edwin Drood	*Gaumont*	(1)(N)
May 1909	Oliver Twist	*Vitagraph*	(1)(N)
May 1909	The Cricket on the Hearth	*Biograph*	(1)(S)
1909	A Knight for a Night *(The Pickwick Papers)*	*Edison*	(1)(N)
Jan 1910	The Dream of Old Scrooge *(A Christmas Carol)*	*Cines*	(X)(S)
Apr 1910	A Yorkshire School *(Nicholas Nickleby)*	*Edison*	(1)(N)
Apr 1910	Oliver Twist	*Film d'Art*	(1)(N)
1910	Oliver Twist	*Denmark*	(1)(N)
Aug 1910	Love and the Law *(David Copperfield)*	*Edison*	(1)(N)
Sep 1910	Jo, the Crossing Sweeper *(Bleak House)*	*Walturdaw*	(1)(N)
Dec 1910	A Christmas Carol	*Edison*	(1)(S)
Jan 1911	The Old Curiosity Shop	*Thanhouser*	(3)(N)
Feb 1911	A Tale of Two Cities	*Vitagraph*	(2)(N)
Mar 1911	How Bella Was Won *(Our Mutual Friend)*	*Edison*	(1)(N)
Sep 1911	The Early Life of David Copperfield *(David Copperfield)*	*Thanhouser*	(1)(N)

Sep 1911	Little Emily and David Copperfield *(David Copperfield)*	*Thanhouser*	(1)(N)
Sep 1911	The Loves of David Copperfield *(David Copperfield)*	*Thanhouser*	(1)(N)
Oct 1911	Little Emily *(David Copperfield)*	*Britannia*	(1)(N)
Dec 1911	Eugene Wrayburn *(Our Mutual Friend)*	*Edison*	(1)(N)
1911	Oliver Twist	*Cines*	(1)(N)
Jan 1912	Leaves from the Books of Charles Dickens	*Britannia*	(1)(N)
Jan 1912	Martin Chuzzlewit	*Edison*	(3)(N)
Mar 1912	Nicholas Nickleby	*Thanhouser*	(2)(N)
Mar 1912	The Old Curiosity Shop	*Britannia*	(1)(N)
May 1912	Oliver Twist	*General*	(5)(N)
May 1912	The Mystery of Edwin Drood	*Film d'Art*	(2)(N)
Aug 1912	Mr Pickwick's Predicament *(The Pickwick Papers)*	*Edison*	(1)(N)
Sep 1912	Oliver Twist	*Hepworth*	(4)(N)
Oct 1912	Mrs Lirriper's Lodgers	*Vitagraph*	(1)(S)
Feb 1913	The Honourable Event *(The Pickwick Papers)*	*Vitagraph*	(1)(N)
Feb 1913	The Adventure of Westgate Seminary *(The Pickwick Papers)*	*Vitagraph*	(1)(N)
Feb 1913	The Adventure of the Shooting Party *(The Pickwick Papers)*	*Vitagraph*	(1)(N)
Jul 1913	Little Dorrit	*Thanhouser*	(2)(N)
Aug 1913	Horatio Sparkins *(Sketches by Boz)*	*Vitagraph*	(1)(S)
Aug 1913	Dolly Varden *(Barnaby Rudge)*	*Edison*	(1)(N)
Sep 1913	David Copperfield	*Hepworth*	(8)(N)
Sep 1913	Scrooge *(A Christmas Carol)*	*Zenith*	(2)(S)
Nov 1913	Pickwick versus Bardell *(The Pickwick Papers)*	*Clarendon*	(1)(N)
Nov 1913	Mr Pickwick in a Double-bedded Room *(The Pickwick Papers)*	*Clarendon*	(1)(N)

Nov 1913	Mrs Corney Makes the Tea *(The Pickwick Papers)*	*Clarendon*	(1)(N)
Dec 1913	The Old Curiosity Shop	*Hepworth*	(5)(N)
Feb 1914	The Cricket on the Hearth	*American*	(2)(N)
Aug 1914	The Cricket on the Hearth	*Biograph*	(2)(S)
Aug 1914	The Chimes	*Hepworth*	(2)(S)
Sep 1914	The Chimes	*World*	(5)(S)
Oct 1914	The Mystery of Edwin Drood	*Blaché*	(5)(N)
Oct 1914	Martin Chuzzlewit	*Biograph*	(2)(N)
Nov 1914	A Christmas Carol	*London*	(1)(S)
Jan 1915	Barnaby Rudge	*Hepworth*	(5)(N)
Sep 1915	Hard Times	*Transatlantic*	(4)(N)
1915	The Cricket on the Hearth	*Thiemann*	(2)(S)

210 DICKEY, Paul (*see also* Goddard)

Nov 1914	The Man from the Sea	*Lubin*	(2)(P)
Dec 1914	The Ghost Breaker	*Lasky*	(5)(P)
Dec 1915	The Misleading Lady	*Essanay*	(P)

211 DICKINSON, Thomas W.

Apr 1915	The Unbroken Road	*Life Photo*	(5)(N)

212 DICKSON, Harris

Jun 1914	The Kangaroo	*Éclair*	(5)(N)

213 DILLENBACK, George P.

Nov 1912	The Mills of the Gods	*Vitagraph*	(3)(N)
Jul 1915	The Price for Folly	*Vitagraph*	(5)(N)

214 DIRKS, Rudolph

May 1903	The Katzenjammer Kids Have a Love Affair	*Biograph*	(X)(C)

Jul 1903	The Katzenjammer Kids and the Schoolmarm	*Biograph*	(X)(C)
Apr 1912	The Katzenjammer Kids	*Selig*	(X)(C)
May 1912	They Go Tobogganing	*Selig*	(X)(C)
May 1912	They Plan a Trip to Germany	*Selig*	(X)(C)
May 1912	They Entertain Company	*Selig*	(X)(C)
Jun 1912	They Go to School	*Selig*	(X)(C)
Jun 1912	Schooldays	*Selig*	(X)(C)
Jun 1912	They Corrupt the School	*Selig*	(X)(C)
Jun 1912	The Arrival of Cousin Otto	*Selig*	(X)(C)

215 DITRICHSTEIN, Leo

Mar 1915	Are You a Mason?	*Famous Players*	(5)(P)

216 DIXON, Thomas

Mar 1915	The Birth of a Nation *(The Clansman)*	*Epoch*	(N)

DODGSON, Charles Lutwidge *see* Carroll

217 DONIZETTI, Gaetano (*see also* Scott, Sir Walter)

Dec 1908	Lucia di Lammermoor	*Itala*	(X)(O)
1908	Lucia di Lammermoor	*Ambrosio*	(X)(O)

218 DONNELL, Annie Hamilton

Dec 1914	'Twas the Night Before Christmas	*Edison*	(1)(Pm)

219 DONNELLY, H. Grattan

Oct 1914	The Ragged Earl (*see also* Humphreys; Lacey)	*Popular*	(4)(N)
1915	Darkest Russia	*Brady*	(5)(P)

Nov 1915	The End of the Road	*American*	(5)(N)

220 DOYLE, Sir Arthur Conan

Feb 1903	Sherlock Holmes Baffled	*Biograph*	(X)(Ch)
Dec 1905	Sherlock Holmes Held for Ransom *(The Sign of the Four)*	*Urban*	(X)(N)
Sep 1905	The Adventures of Sherlock Holmes *(The Sign of the Four)*	*Vitagraph*	(X)(N)
1908	Sherlock Holmes	*Nordisk*	(1)(S)
Nov 1908	Sherlock Holmes in the Great Murder Mystery	*Crescent*	(1)(Ch)
Jan 1909	Sherlock Holmes No. 2	*Nordisk*	(1)(Ch)
Jun 1909	Sherlock Holmes: Cab No. 519	*Nordisk*	(1)(Ch)
Oct 1909	The Latest Triumph of Sherlock Holmes	*Gaumont*	(1)(Ch)
Nov 1910	The Bogus Governess	*Nordisk*	(1)(Ch)
Dec 1910	The Stolen Legacy	*Nordisk*	(1)(Ch)
Dec 1910	The Hotel Thieves	*Nordisk*	(1)(Ch)
Nov 1912	The Speckled Band	*Éclair*	(2)(S)
Nov 1912	Silver Blaze	*Éclair*	(1)(S)
Dec 1912	The Beryl Coronet	*Éclair*	(2)(S)
Dec 1912	The Musgrave Ritual	*Éclair*	(1)(S)
Jan 1913	The Reigate Squires	*Éclair*	(2)(S)
Jan 1913	The Stolen Papers	*Éclair*	(1)(S)
Feb 1913	The Mystery of Boscombe Vale	*Éclair*	(2)(S)
Feb 1913	The Copper Beeches	*Éclair*	(2)(S)
Feb 1913	Sherlock Holmes Solves the Sign of Four *(The Sign of the Four)*	*Thanhouser*	(2)(N)
Sep 1913	The House of Temperley *(Rodney Stone)*	*London*	(4)(N)
1914	The Hound of the Baskervilles	*Pathé*	(4)(N)
Oct 1914	A Study in Scarlet	*Samuelson*	(6)(N)
Dec 1914	A Study in Scarlet	*Universal*	(2)(N)
Sep 1915	Brigadier Gerard *(The Exploits of Brigadier Gerard)*	*Barker*	(5)(N)
Dec 1915	The Firm of Girdlestone	*London*	(6)(N)

221 DREW, John

Dec 1915	Rosemary	*Quality*	(5)(N)

222 DREW, Sidney

Sep 1911	The Red Devils *(The Red Man)*	*Champion*	(1)(S)

223 DUCKWORTH, Madge

May 1915	Her Nameless Child	*B & C*	(3)(N)

DUDEVANT, Amandine Aurore *see* Sand

224 DUMAS, Alexandre (Dumas *père*)

Aug 1898	The Corsican Brothers	*Smith*	(X)(N)
Sep 1898	Fencing Contest From 'The Three Musketeers' *(The Three Musketeers)*	*Biograph*	(X)(N)
Nov 1902	The Corsican Brothers	*Harrison*	(X)(N)
Feb 1908	The Count of Monte Cristo	*Selig*	(1)(N)
Dec 1908	The Three Musketeers	*Cines*	(1)(N)
1908	The Prisoner of the Château d'If *(The Count of Monte Cristo)*	*Éclair*	(1)(N)
Feb 1909	The Lady of Monsoreau *(La Dame de Monsoreau)*	*Cines*	(1)(N)
Mar 1909	The Man in the Iron Mask	*Itala*	(1)(N)
May 1909	The Tower of Nesle	*Pathé*	(1)(N)
1909	Don César de Bazan	*Éclair*	(1)(N)
Mar 1910	The Count of Monte Cristo	*Challenge*	(1)(N)
Apr 1910	Kean, or the Prince and the Actor	*Nordisk*	(1)(P)
Jan 1911	The Count of Monte Cristo	*Powers*	(1)(N)
Sep 1911	The Three Musketeers	*Edison*	(1)(N)
Feb 1912	The Corsican Brothers	*Edison*	(1)(N)
Aug 1912	The Count of Monte Cristo	*Selig*	(3)(N)
1912	The Tower of Nesle	*SCAGL*	(3)(N)

1913	The Lady of Monsoreau	*Éclair*	(7)(N)
1913	Le Chevalier de Maison-Rouge	*SCAGL*	(3)(N)
Dec 1913	The Three Musketeers	*Film d'Art*	(7)(N)
Jan 1914	Chicot the Jester *(La Dame de Monsoreau)*	*Éclair*	(3)(N)
Feb 1914	The Three Musketeers	*Anglo*	(N)
Apr 1914	The Three Musketeers	*Cosmos*	(N)
Jul 1914	The Reign of Terror	*Eclectic*	(4)(N)
1914	Monte Cristo *(The Count of Monte Cristo)*	*Film d'Art*	(7)(N)
Dec 1914	Queen Margaret *(La Reine Margot)*	*SCAGL*	(N)
Apr 1915	The Corsican Brothers	*Universal*	(5)(N)
1915	The Corsican Brothers	*SCAGL*	(N)

225 DUMAS, Alexandre (Dumas *fils*)

Mar 1908	The Lady with the Camellias *(La Dame aux Camélias)*	*Nordisk*	(1)(P)
Sep 1909	The Lady with the Camellias *(La Dame aux Camélias)*	*Film d'Art*	(1)(P)
Apr 1910	The Miner and Camille *(La Dame aux Camélias)*	*Edison*	(X)(N)
1911	La Dame aux Camélias	*Film d'Art*	(2)(P)
Jun 1912	Camille *(La Dame aux Camélias)*	*Champion*	(1)(N)
1914	Denise	*Film d'Art*	(4)(P)
Jul 1915	The Clemenceau Case	*Fox*	(6)(N)
Dec 1915	Camille *(La Dame aux Camélias)*	*Shubert*	(4)(N)

226 DU MAURIER, George

Dec 1896	Trilby and Little Billee *(Trilby)*	*Biograph*	(X)(N)
May 1908	Trilby	*Nordisk*	(X)(N)
1910	Trilby	*Kinemacolor*	(1)(N)
Jan 1912	Trilby	*Ouki*	(N)
1912	Trilby	*Biograph*	(N)

1912	Trilby	*Standard*	(N)
Apr 1913	Trilby	*Famous Players*	(4)(N)
May 1914	Svengali der Hypnotiser *(Trilby)*	*Weiner*	(1)(N)
Jun 1914	Trilby	*London*	(3)(N)
Aug 1915	Trilby	*Equitable*	(4)(N)

227 DU MAURIER, Guy

Sep 1914	An Englishman's Home	*B & C*	(2)(P)

DUNKERLEY, William Arthur *see* Oxenham

DUPIN, Amandine Aurore *see* Sand

228 DURANT, Harold Riggs

Jul 1914	Moonshine Molly	*Majestic*	(2)(S)
Apr 1915	A Man and His Mate	*Reliance*	(4)(N)

229 DU SOUCHET, Henry A.

Dec 1914	Who Goes There?	*Edison*	(2)(P)
Nov 1914	The Man From Mexico	*Famous Players*	(5)(P)
Aug 1915	My Friend from India	*Edison*	(3)(P)

230 DWYER, James Francis

Nov 1913	The Girl in the Houseboat *(Mr Leander)*	*Edison*	(1)(S)
Oct 1915	The Spider	*Essanay*	(2)(S)

231 ECHEGARAY, José

Jan 1915	The World and His Wife *(El Gran Galeoto)*	*Box Office*	(5)(Pm)

232 EDMONDS, E. Vivian

Jul 1914	The King's Romance *(see also* Austin*)*	*B & C*	(4)(P)

233 EDWARDS, Gus

Dec 1907	Schooldays	*Kalem*	(X)(P)

234 EGGLESTON, Edward

Oct 1914	The Hoosier Schoolmaster	*Masterpiece*	(5)(N)

235 ELIOT, George (Marian Evans, later Cross)

Sep 1909	A Fair Exchange *(Silas Marner)*	*Biograph*	(1)(N)
Dec 1910	Romola	*Cines*	(1)(N)
Apr 1911	Silas Marner	*Thanhouser*	(1)(N)
Oct 1913	Silas Marner	*Edison*	(2)(N)
Sep 1914	Gwendolen *(Daniel Deronda)*	*Biograph*	(2)(N)
Apr 1915	Adam Bede	*Biograph*	(3)(N)
May 1915	Felix Holt	*Biograph*	(2)(N)
Dec 1915	The Mill on the Floss	*Thanhouser*	(5)(N)
Dec 1915	Silas Marner	*Thanhouser*	(4)(N)

236 ELLIS, John Breckenridge

Oct 1915	Emmy of Stork's Nest *(Stork's Nest)*	*Metro*	(5)(N)

237 EMERSON, John

Dec 1914	The Conspiracy *(see also* Baker*)*	*Famous Players*	(4)(P)

238 ERASTOV, George

Aug 1915 Sold — *Famous Players* (5)(N)
(*see also* Bernstein)

239 ERCKMANN, Émile (*see also* Chatrian)

Feb 1913 The Bells — *Reliance* (2)(P)
(*Le Juif Polonais*)
Jun 1914 The Bells — *Australia* (4)(P)
(*Le Juif Polonais*)

240 ESMOND, Henry V.

Apr 1915 When We Were Twenty-one — *Famous Players* (4)(N)

241 EVANS, Ida M.

Apr 1914 A Question of Hats and Gowns — *Edison* (2)(S)
(*Town Pumps and Gold Leaf*)

EVANS, Marian *see* Eliot

242 EVANS, Will

May 1913 Harnessing a Horse — *Hepworth* (1)(P)
Dec 1914 Building a Chicken House — *Sunny South* (1)(P)
Dec 1914 The Jockey — *Sunny South* (1)(P)
Dec 1914 Moving a Piano — *Sunny South* (1)(P)
Dec 1914 The Showman's Dream — *Sunny South* (1)(P)
Dec 1914 Tincture of Iron — *Sunny South* (1)(P)

243 EWERS, Hanns Heinz

Nov 1913 The Student of Prague — *Bioskop* (4)(N)
Aug 1914 The Eyes of Old Brandeis — *Bioskop* (4)(N)

244 FAGAN, James Bernard

Jan 1914 The Wheel of Life — *Nestor* (1)(S)

Nov 1915 Bella Donna *Famous Players* (5)(P)
(*see also* Hichens)

245 FAIRFAX, Marion

Dec 1915 The Immigrant *Lasky* (5)(N)

FARGUS, Frederick *see* Conway

246 FARLEY, Ellen

Nov 1914 The Folly of Anne *Majestic* (1)(S)

247 FAUCHOIS, René

1912 The Empress Josephine *Film d'Art* (1)(P)

248 FERGUSON, William Blair Morton

Sep 1914 Face Value *Edison* (2)(S)
Oct 1914 Garrison's Finish *Selig* (3)(N)

249 FEUILLET, Octave

Dec 1914 The Romance of a Poor Young Man *Biograph* (2)(S)
(Le Roman d'un Jeune Homme Pauvre)

250 FÉVAL, Paul

Dec 1912 The Hunchback *Union* (3)(N)
(Le Jeunesse du Bossu)

251 FEYDEAU, Georges

Oct 1912 The Girl from Maxim's *Éclair* (2)(P)
(La Dame de chez Maxim's)
1913 Le Dindon *Film d'Art* (2)(P)

252 FIELD, Eugene

Jan 1912	Little Boy Blue	*Powers*	(1)(Pm)
Jun 1914	The Dream Ship	*Beauty*	(1)(Pm)

253 FILES, Franklyn

Jan 1915	The Girl I Left Behind Me (*see also* Belasco)	*Box Office*	(5)(P)

254 FINNEGAN, Mulloy

Jan 1915	Out of the Storm	*Lubin*	(1)(S)

255 FISHER, Harry Conway (Bud)

Jun 1911	Mutt and Jeff on the Job	*Nestor*	(X)(C)
Jul 1911	Mutt Joins the Force	*Nestor*	(X)(C)
Aug 1911	Mutt and Jeff and the Goldstein Burglars	*Nestor*	(X)(C)
Sep 1911	Mutt and Jeff and the Escaped Lunatic	*Nestor*	(X)(C)
Sep 1911	Mutt and Jeff and the Newsboys	*Nestor*	(X)(C)
Sep 1911	Mutt and Jeff and the Dogcatchers	*Nestor*	(X)(C)
Sep 1911	Mutt and Jeff as Reporters	*Nestor*	(X)(C)
Oct 1911	Mutt and Jeff Spend a Quiet Day in the Country	*Nestor*	(X)(C)
Oct 1911	Mutt and Jeff and the Black Hand	*Nestor*	(X)(C)
Oct 1911	Mutt and Jeff Join the Opera Company	*Nestor*	(X)(C)
Oct 1911	Mutt and Jeff Discover a Wonderful Remedy	*Nestor*	(X)(C)
Nov 1911	Mutt and Jeff and the Unlucky Star	*Nestor*	(X)(C)
Nov 1911	Mutt's Scheme That Failed	*Nestor*	(X)(C)
Nov 1911	Mutt and Jeff Make the Feathers Fly	*Nestor*	(X)(C)
Nov 1911	Mutt and Jeff Break into Society	*Nestor*	(X)(C)
Nov 1911	Mutt and Jeff and the Lady Stenographer	*Nestor*	(X)(C)
Dec 1911	Mutt and Jeff and the Italian Strikers	*Nestor*	(X)(C)
Dec 1911	Mutt and Jeff Fall in Love	*Nestor*	(X)(C)

256 FISKE, Harrison Grey

Jan 1915	The District Attorney	*Lubin*	(4)(P)
	(See also Klein*)*		

257 FITCH, Clyde

Aug 1911	The Battle of Bunker Hill	*Edison*	(1)(P)
Nov 1914	The Straight Road	*Famous Players*	(5)(P)
April 1915	The Cowboy and the Lady	*Rolfe*	(5)(P)
May 1915	The Moth and the Flame	*Famous Players*	(5)(P)
May 1915	Her Own Way	*Popular*	(5)(P)
May 1915	The Stubbornness of Geraldine	*Art*	(5)(P)
May 1915	The Climbers	*Lubin*	(5)(P)
Aug 1915	The Second in Command	*Quality*	(5)(P)
Sep 1915	Her Great Match	*Popular*	(5)(P)
Dec 1915	Barbara Frietchie	*Popular*	(5)(P)
	(See also Whittier*)*		
Dec 1915	Captain Jinks of the Horse Marines	*Essanay*	(5)(P)

258 FITCH, George

May 1912	A Funeral That Flashed in the Pan	*Edison*	(1)(S)
Jul 1912	Their Hero	*Edison*	(1)(S)

259 FLAGG, James Montgomery

Oct 1914	The Adventures of Kitty Cobb	*Colonial*	(4)(C)

260 FLAUBERT, Gustave

Jun 1911	Salammbô	*Ambrosio*	(1)(N)
Sep 1914	Salammbô	*Pasquali*	(4)(N)
Mar 1915	Salammbô	*World*	(5)(N)

261 FLEMING, Carroll

Aug 1915	The Master Hand	*Premo*	(5)(N)

262 FLEXNER, Anne Crawford

Dec 1914	Mrs Wiggs of the Cabbage Patch	*California*	(5)(N)
	(see also Rice*)*		

FLOTOW *see* Von Flotow

263 FOOTNER, Hulbert

Mar 1915	Jack Chanty	*Masterpiece*	(5)(N)
Aug 1915	Sealed Valley	*Metro*	(5)(N)

264 FORBES, James

Apr 1915	The Commuters	*Kleine*	(5)(P)
Oct 1915	The Chorus Lady	*Lasky*	(5)(P)

265 FORD, F. G.

Dec 1912	An Old-fashioned Elopement	*Edison*	(1)(S)

266 FORMAN, Justus Miles

Jan 1915	The Garden of Lies	*All Star*	(5)(N)

267 FOUQUÉ, Friedrich de la Motte

Feb 1910	Undine	*Cines*	(1)(N)
Sep 1912	Undine	*Thanhouser*	(2)(N)
Sep 1912	Neptune's Daughter *(Undine)*	*Essanay*	(1)(N)
Dec 1915	Undine	*Bluebird*	(5)(N)

268 FOX, John William, Jr

May 1914	The Trail of the Lonesome Pine *(see also Walter)*	*Broadway*	(5)(N)

269 FRANCE, Anatole (Jacques-Anatole-François Thibault)

Nov 1914	Thaïs	*Loftus*	(4)(N)

FRANKAU, Julia Davis *see* Dauby

270 FRANKLIN, Edgar Stearns (Edgar Franklin Stearns)

Aug 1914	The Motor Buccaneers	*Essanay*	(2)(S)
Aug 1914	Seven Sealed Orders	*Essanay*	(2)(S)
Sep 1915	Postponed	*Vitagraph*	(5)(N)

271 FREDERICKS, Arnold (Frederic Arnold Kummer)

Nov 1915	One Million Dollars *(One Million Francs)*	*Rolfe*	(5)(N)

272 FRENCH, Herbert

May 1913	The Poet and the Soldier *(Apollo and the Seaman)(see also* Trench*)*	*Kalem*	(1)(S)

273 FROST, Arthur Burdett

Nov 1914	Dizzy Joe's Career	*Komic*	(1)(C)

274 FROST, Walter Archer

Jul 1914	A Red Man's Heart	*Majestic*	(1)(S)

275 FULDA, Ludwig

Aug 1914	The Lost Paradise *(see also* De Mille, Henry Churchill*)*	*Famous Players*	(5)(P)

276 FULLERTON, Hugh S.

Jun 1912	The High Cost of Living *(Bacon Dull, Love Active and Strong)*	*Edison*	(1)(S)

277 FURNESS, Edith Ellis

Jul 1915	Seven Sisters	*Famous Players*	(5)(N)

278 FURNISS, Grace Livingstone

Feb 1914	The Pride of Jennico (*see also* Richardson)	*Famous Players*	(5)(P)
Mar 1915	Gretna Green	*Famous Players*	(5)(P)
Sep 1915	On with the Dance	*Vitagraph*	(5)(P)

279 FUTRELLE, Jacques

Jan 1914	A Model Young Man	*Vitagraph*	(4)(N)
Jul 1914	Adventures in Diplomacy (*Elusive Isabel*)	*Éclair*	(3)(N)
Aug 1914	The Painted World	*Vitagraph*	(3)(N)
Mar 1915	The High Hand	*Favorite*	(5)(N)

280 FUTRELLE, May

Jul 1915	The Secretary of Frivolous Affairs	*American*	(5)(N)

281 GABORIAU, Émile

Sep 1914	Monsieur Lecoq	*Éclair*	(3)(N)
Jan 1915	File No. 113	*Biograph*	(2)(N)

282 GABRIEL

Oct 1913	The Master Rogue	*Éclair*	(3)(N)

283 GALLAND, Seymour

Nov 1914	Who Was Who in Hog's Hollow	*Vitagraph*	(1)(S)
Nov 1915	Heredity	*Vitagraph*	(3)(N)

284 GALLON, Tom

Mar 1913	The Man from Outside	*Reliance*	(3)(N)
Nov 1915	The Man in Motley	*London*	(3)(N)

285 GALOPIN, Arnold

Jun 1914	The Mystery of Green Park	*Éclipse*	(2)(S)

286 GANTHONY, Richard

Aug 1913	A Message from Mars	*UK*	(4)(P)

287 GARRICK, David

Jun 1915	The Country Girl	*Thanhouser*	(2)(P)

288 GARVICE, Charles

Aug 1915	The Verdict of the Heart	*Clarendon*	(3)(N)

289 GATES, Eleanor

Oct 1914	Doc	*Sawyer*	(3)(N)

290 GAUTIER, Théophile

Jan 1909	Cleopatra's Lover	*Vitagraph*	(1)(S)
Dec 1910	The Romance of the Mummy	*Pathé*	(1)(N)
May 1915	Captain Fracasse	*Biograph*	(4)(N)

291 GEMELLI, Enrico

Jan 1914	The Heart of a Police Officer	*World*	(4)(N)

292 GEOFFREYS, Oliver M. (Eve Unsell)

Dec 1915	The Ransom *(The Marionettes)*	*Triumph*	(5)(N)

293 GEOFFROY, Gustave

Jan 1914 The Horrors of War *Éclair* (3)(N)
(L'Apprenti)

294 GERARD, Rosemonde

Feb 1914 A Good Little Devil *Famous Players* (5)(N)
(see also Rostand, Maurice; Strong*)*

295 GERMAINE, Mary

Dec 1914 Wildflower *Famous Players* (4)(N)

296 GIBSON, Charles Dana

Nov 1914 The Education of Mr Pipp *All Star* (5)(C)
(see also Thomas, Augustus*)*

297 GILBERT, Sir William Schwenck

May 1907 The Mikado *Gaumont* (X)(O)
(see also Sullivan*)*

Jul 1907 The Mikado *Walturdaw* (X)(O)
(see also Sullivan*)*

Aug 1907 The Yeomen of the Guard *Walturdaw* (X)(O)
(see also Sullivan*)*

Mar 1912 The Yarn of the 'Nancy Belle' *Edison* (1)(Pm)

May 1913 The Yarn of the 'Nancy Belle' *Lubin* (1)(Pm)

298 GILLMORE, Rufus

Nov 1915 The Alster Case *Essanay* (5)(N)

299 GILMORE, Barney

May 1913	Kelly from the Emerald Isle *(see also* McCullough*)*	*Solax*	(1)(Sg)

300 GINNETT, Fred

Apr 1906	Dick Turpin's Last Ride to York	*Warwick*	(X)(P)

301 GLYN, Elinor

Jan 1915	Three Weeks	*Reliable*	(5)(N)

302 GODDARD, Charles William (*see also* Dickey)

Nov 1914	The Man from the Sea	*Lubin*	(2)(P)
Dec 1914	The Ghost Breaker	*Lasky*	(5)(P)
Dec 1915	The Misleading Lady	*Essanay*	(5)(P)

303 GOETHE, Johann Wolfgang Von

1898	Faust	*Lumière*	(X)(P)
1898	The Damnation of Faust *(Faust)*	*Méliès*	(X)(P)
Aug 1898	Faust and Mephistopheles *(Faust)*	*Smith*	(X)(P)
Feb 1900	Faust and Marguerite *(Faust)*	*Edison*	(X)(P)
Dec 1903	The Damnation of Faust *(Faust)*	*Méliès*	(1)(P)
1907	Faust	*Gaumont*	(1)(P)
Apr 1909	The Damnation of Faust *(Faust)*	*Méliès*	(1)(P)
May 1909	Mephisto and the Maiden *(Faust)*	*Selig*	(1)(P)

Dec 1909	Faust	*Edison*	(1)(P)
Feb 1910	Werther *(The Sorrows of Young Werther)*	*Film d'Art*	(1)(N)
1910	Faust	*Éclair*	(1)(P)
Jan 1910	Faust	*Animatophone*	(1)(O)
Apr 1910	Faust	*Cines*	(1)(P)
Apr 1910	Faust and Marguerite *(Faust)*	*Gaumont*	(1)(O)
Aug 1910	Cagliostro	*Pathé*	(1)(N)
Aug 1910	Faust	*Pathé*	(2)(P)
Apr 1911	Faust	*Hepworth*	(1)(O)
Jan 1912	Mignon, or the Child of Fate *(Wilhelm Meister)(see also* Thomas, Ambroise*)*	*Solax*	(1)(N)
Jan 1915	Mignon *(Wilhelm Meister)(see also* Kenyon*)*	*California*	(5)(N)

304 GOLDSMITH, Oliver

Aug 1910	She Stoops to Conquer	*Thanhouser*	(1)(P)
Dec 1910	The Vicar of Wakefield	*Thanhouser*	(1)(N)
Jan 1912	The Vicar of Wakefield	*Britannia*	(1)(N)
Sep 1913	The Vicar of Wakefield	*Planet*	(3)(N)
Sep 1913	The Vicar of Wakefield	*Hepworth*	(3)(N)
Feb 1914	She Stoops to Conquer	*London*	(3)(P)
1915	The Minister *(The Vicar of Wakefield)*	*Eastern*	(5)(N)

305 GOLLAN, Campbell

Dec 1915	Wild Oats *(see also* White, John*)*	*Kleine*	(5)(N)

306 GOODHUE, Willis M.

Sep 1915	The Fixer *(Hello, Bill)*	*Kleine*	(5)(N)

307 GOODMAN, Daniel Carson

Feb 1914	The Green-eyed Devil	*Reliance*	(2)(N)
Apr 1914	The Battle of the Sexes *(The Single Standard)*	*Mutual*	(5)(N)
Feb 1915	Imar the Servitor	*Majestic*	(4)(N)
Sep 1915	The Silent Accuser	*Lubin*	(1)(S)
Oct 1915	The Orgy	*Lubin*	(1)(S)
Oct 1915	The Son	*Lubin*	(1)(S)
Oct 1915	Think, Mothers	*Lubin*	(2)(S)
Oct 1915	When Youth Is Ambitious	*Lubin*	(2)(S)
Dec 1915	Heartaches	*Lubin*	(4)(N)
Dec 1915	Beyond All Is Love	*Lubin*	(3)(N)

308 GOODMAN, Jules Eckert

Sep 1914	Mother	*Brady*	(4)(N)
May 1915	Two Natures Within Him	*Selig*	(4)(N)
Sep 1915	The Silent Voice	*Quality*	(5)(N)

309 GORDIN, Jacob

Jul 1915	The Kreutzer Sonata (*see also* Tolstoi)	*Fox*	(5)(N)

310 GOSS, Charles Frederick

Apr 1914	The Redemption of David Corson	*Famous Players*	(4)(N)

311 GOULD, Nat

1909	The Double Event	*Tait*	(1)(N)

GRAVES, Clotilda Inez Mary *see* Dehan

312 GRAY, George

Dec 1912	The Fighting Parson (*see also* Davis, Christopher)	*Barker*	(3)(P)
Dec 1913	The Road to Ruin	*Barker*	(4)(P)

313 GRAY, Maxwell (Mary Gleed Tuttiett)

1914	The Silence of Dean Maitland	*Fraser*	(4)(N)
Nov 1915	The Reproach of Annesley	*Biograph*	(4)(N)
Dec 1915	Sealed Lips *(The Silence of Dean Maitland)*	*Equitable*	(5)(N)

314 GRAY, Thomas

Oct 1913	The Restless Spirit *(Elegy in a Country Churchyard)*	*Victor*	(3)(Pm)

315 GRAY, William B.

Dec 1913	The Volunteer Organist	*Gray*	(8)(N)

316 GRAYDON, W. Murray

Oct 1909	Sexton Blake *(Five Years After)(see also* Denton; Meredith, Hal*)*	*Gaumont*	(1)(N)

317 GREEN, Anna Katherine

May 1915	The Millionaire Baby	*Selig*	(5)(N)
Jun 1915	A Strange Disappearance	*Imp*	(N)

318 GREEN, Thomas

Jul 1898	The Policeman, the Cook and the Copper *(The Area Belle)*	*Smith*	(X)(P)

319 GREY, Harold

Jul 1915	The Man Who Stayed at Home *(see also* Worrall*)*	*Hepworth*	(3)(P)

320 GRIMM, Jakob and Wilhelm

1901	Little Red Riding Hood	*Méliès*	(X)(S)

1901	Bluebeard	*Méliès*	(X)(S)
Oct 1907	The Babes in the Wood	*Miles*	(1)(S)
Oct 1909	Hansel and Gretel	*Edison*	(X)(S)
Feb 1910	The Little Old Men of the Woods *(Snow White)*	*Kalem*	(1)(S)
Mar 1910	Little Snowdrop	*Pathé*	(1)(S)
Nov 1911	Little Red Riding Hood	*Essanay*	(1)(S)
Dec 1911	Little Red Riding Hood	*Majestic*	(1)(S)
Jan 1913	Snow White	*Powers*	(3)(S)

321 GUEST, Edgar Albert

Nov 1915	The Reform Candidate *(see also* Arbuckle*)*	*Pallas*	(5)(Pm)

322 GUIMERA, Angel

Oct 1914	Marta of the Lowlands	*Famous Players*	(5)(N)

323 GUNTER, Archibald Clavering

Apr 1914	Mr Barnes of New York	*Vitagraph*	(5)(N)
Aug 1914	My Official Wife *(see also* Savage*)*	*Vitagraph*	(5)(N)
Sep 1914	A Florida Enchantment	*Vitagraph*	(5)(N)
Dec 1914	The Man Behind the Door	*Vitagraph*	(4)(N)
Dec 1915	The Surprises of an Empty Hotel	*Vitagraph*	(5)(N)

GUTHRIE, Thomas Anstey *see* Anstey

324 GUTZKOW, Karl F.

May 1914	Uriel Acosta	*Great Players*	(5)(N)

325 GYP (Marie-Antoinette de Riquetti de Mirabeau)

Apr 1914	The Sparrow	*Leading Players*	(3)(S)
Jun 1914	Soeurette's Sacrifice	*Éclair*	(2)(S)

326 HABBERTON, John

Sep 1915	Helen's Babies	*Thanhouser*	(5)(N)

327 HACKETT, Walter

Sep 1915	Regeneration *(see also* Kildare)	*Fox*	(5)(P)

328 HAGGARD, Sir Henry Rider

1899	The Pillar of Fire *(She)*	*Méliès*	(X)(N)
Nov 1908	She	*Edison*	(1)(N)
May 1911	She	*Thanhouser*	(2)(N)
May 1912	Jess	*Thanhouser*	(3)(N)
Feb 1914	Jess	*Kennedy*	(4)(N)
Nov 1915	Mr Meeson's Will *(John Meeson's Will)*	*Thanhouser*	(4)(N)

329 HALE, Edward Everett

Jun 1909	The Man without a Country	*Edison*	(1)(S)
Feb 1912	My Double and How He Undid Me	*Edison*	(1)(S)

330 HALL, Owen

Aug 1897	Mountainous *(The Geisha)*	*Paul*	(X)(P)
Aug 1897	The Marquis *(The Geisha)*	*Paul*	(X)(P)

331 HALM, Friedrich

Sep 1908	Ingomar *(Son of the Wilderness)*	*Edison*	(1)(P)
Oct 1908	The Barbarian Ingomar *(Son of the Wilderness)*	*Biograph*	(1)(P)

332 HALSEY, Forrest

Jan 1913	The Open Road	*Reliance*	(1)(S)
Apr 1913	A Study in Sociology	*Majestic*	(1)(S)
Apr 1913	The Bawler Out	*Reliance*	(1)(S)
May 1913	The Children of Saint Anne	*Majestic*	(1)(S)
Jun 1914	The Stain	*Eclectic*	(6)(N)

333 HAMEL, Richard

Oct 1908	David Garrick	*Edison*	(1)(P)

334 HAMILTON, Cosmo

Jul 1915	The Blindness of Virtue	*Essanay*	(4)(N)

335 HAMILTON, Henry (*see also* Raleigh)

May 1915	The Great Ruby	*Lubin*	(4)(P)
Jul 1915	The Derby Winner	*London*	(5)(P)
Dec 1915	The Sins of Society	*Brady*	(5)(P)

336 HANLON BROTHERS

Oct 1914	Fantasma	*Edison*	(4)(P)

337 HANNAN, Charles

Sep 1915	A Cigarette Maker's Romance	*Hepworth*	(4)(P)

338 HANSHEW, Thomas W.

Apr 1911	Monsieur	*Edison*	(1)(S)
May 1911	A Case of High Treason *(The Under Man)*	*Edison*	(1)(S)
Jun 1911	His Misjudgement *(Purple and Fine Linen)*	*Edison*	(1)(S)
Nov 1913	The Chronicles of Cleek	*Edison*	(serial)(S)

339 HARDY, Thomas

Sep 1913	Tess of the d'Urbervilles	*Famous Players*	(4)(N)
Nov 1915	Far from the Madding Crowd	*Turner*	(5)(N)

340 HARKINS, James

Aug 1914	Northern Lights *(see also* Barbour*)*	*Life Photo*	(5)(P)

341 HARRIS, Charles Kessell

Jul 1914	After the Ball	*Photodrama*	(6)(P)
Jul 1915	Always in the Way	*Dyreda*	(5)(P)
May 1915	When It Strikes Home	*World*	(5)(P)
Nov 1915	Hearts of Men	*World*	(5)(P)

342 HARRIS, Elmer Blaney

Apr 1915	Pretty Mrs Smith *(see also* Morosco*)*	*Morosco*	(5)(N)
Jun 1915	The Wild Olive *(see also* King; Morosco*)*	*Morosco*	(5)(N)

343 HARRISON, Edith Ogden

Mar 1915	The Lady of the Snows	*Edison*	(3)(N)

344 HARRISON, Frances Burton

Sep 1914	The Unwelcome Mrs Hatch	*Famous Players*	(4)(N)

345 HARRISON, Henry Sydnor

Jul 1915	Captivating Mary Carstairs	*National*	(5)(N)

346 HARTE, Bret

Aug 1908	The Red Man and His Child	*Biograph*	(X)(S)
Sep 1908	The Heart of Oyama	*Biograph*	(X)(S)
Jan 1910	The Luck of Roaring Camp	*Edison*	(X)(S)

Mar 1910	Bradford's Claim	*Edison*	(X)(S)
Oct 1910	Ononko's Vow	*Edison*	(X)(S)
Dec 1910	The Stolen Claim	*Edison*	(1)(S)
1911	The Luck of Roaring Camp	*Johnson*	(1)(S)
May 1911	The White Rose of the Wilds	*Biograph*	(1)(S)
Jul 1911	The Last Drop of Water	*Biograph*	(1)(S)
Dec 1911	The Kid from Roaring Camp *(The Luck of Roaring Camp)*	*Champion*	(1)(S)
Mar 1912	The Goddess of Sagebrush Gulch	*Biograph*	(1)(S)
Oct 1912	In the Aisles of the Wild	*Biograph*	(1)(S)
May 1913	John Burns of Gettysburg	*Kalem*	(1)(S)
May 1914	The Breed of the North	*Broncho*	(2)(S)
Jul 1914	Salomy Jane *(Salomy Jane's Kiss)* (*see also* Armstrong)	*California*	(6)(N)
1914	The Bad Luck of Santa Inez	*Domino*	(2)(S)
Mar 1915	M'Liss	*Shubert*	(5)(N)
Apr 1915	The Lily of Poverty Flat *(Her Letter, His Answer)*	*California*	(5)(N)
Nov 1915	Salomy Jane *(Salomy Jane's Kiss)*	*Alco*	(5)(N)

347 HARVEY, Frank

Jun 1914	Woman Against Woman	*Biograph*	(4)(P)

348 HAUPTMANN, Gerhart Johann Robert

Aug 1913	Atlantis	*Nordisk*	(6)(N)
1913	The Miracle	*Menschen*	(5)(P)

HAWKINS, Sir Anthony Hope *see* Hope

349 HAWTHORNE, Nathaniel

Mar 1908	The Scarlet Letter	*Kalem*	(1)(N)
Dec 1908	Lord Feathertop *(Feathertop)*	*Edison*	(1)(S)

Oct 1910	The House of the Seven Gables	*Edison*	(1)(N)
Apr 1911	The Scarlet Letter	*Imp*	(1)(N)
May 1912	Feathertop	*Éclair*	(1)(S)
Apr 1913	Feathertop	*Kinemacolor*	(2)(S)
May 1913	The Scarlet Letter	*Kinemacolor*	(3)(N)
Jun 1913	The Transgressor *(The Scarlet Letter)*	*Broncho*	(2)(N)
Nov 1915	The New Adam and Eve	*Rialto*	(3)(N)

350 HAY, John G.

Aug 1912	Jim Bludso	*Kalem*	(1)(S)
Apr 1915	Little Breeches	*Lubin*	(1)(S)
Sep 1915	The Blood Seedling	*Selig*	(2)(S)

351 HAYES, J. Milton

Sep 1913	The Green Eye of the Little Yellow God	*Edison*	(1)(Pm)

352 HAZELTINE, Horace (Charles Stokes Wayne)

Nov 1915	The Sable Lorcha	*Fine Arts*	(5)(N)

353 HAZELTON, George C.

Feb 1915	Mistress Nell *(Nell Gwynn)*	*Famous Players*	(5)(P)
Oct 1915	The Raven	*Essanay*	(6)(P)

354 HEIJERMANS, Herman

Dec 1913	A Case of Arson	*Britannic*	(4)(P)

355 HEINE, Heinrich

May 1912	The Pilgrimage	*Kalem*	(1)(S)
Jan 1913	The Lorelei	*Edison*	(1)(Pm)

356 HEMYNG, Bracebridge

Dec 1910	The Childhood of Jack Harkaway *(Jack Harkaway)*	*Thanhouser*	(1)(N)

357 HENDERSON, Isaac

Nov 1915	The Mummy and the Humming Bird	*Famous Players*	(5)(P)

358 HENRY, O. (William Sydney Porter)

Jan 1909	The Sacrifice *(The Gift of the Magi)*	*Biograph*	(1)(S)
May 1909	His Duty	*Biograph*	(X)(S)
Nov 1909	His Masterpiece	*Edison*	(X)(S)
Feb 1911	The Ransom of Red Chief	*Edison*	(1)(S)
Jul 1911	The Trapper's Five-dollar Bill *(The Whirligig of Life)*	*Edison*	(1)(S)
Jan 1912	Thirty Days' Hard Labor *(The Halbardier of the Little Rheinschloss)*	*Edison*	(1)(S)
May 1912	A Western Prince Charming *(A Chapparal Prince)*	*Edison*	(1)(S)
Nov 1912	Friends in San Rosario	*Selig*	(1)(S)
Dec 1912	Pat Clancy's Adventure *(The Shamrock and the Palm)*	*Edison*	(1)(S)
Feb 1913	All on Account of an Egg	*Éclair*	(2)(S)
Feb 1913	Hearts and Crosses	*Éclair*	(2)(S)
Apr 1913	The Splendid Scapegrace *(A Blackjack Bargain)*	*Edison*	(1)(S)
May 1913	The Badge of Policeman O'Roon	*Éclair*	(2)(S)
Sep 1913	The Reformation of Calliope	*Éclair*	(2)(S)
Mar 1914	A Mexican's Gratitude *(A Chapparal Christmas Gift)*	*Edison*	(1)(S)
Apr 1914	The Caballero's Way	*Éclair*	(3)(S)
Jun 1914	The Stirrup Brother	*Éclair*	(2)(S)
Sep 1914	The Saving of Young Anderson	*Reliance*	(2)(S)
Oct 1914	Jimmy Hayes and Muriel	*Selig*	(1)(S)

359 HERBERT, Murray

Mar 1915	The Angel of the Ward	*Barker*	(3)(N)

360 HERI, Henrik

Jul 1913	King René's Daughter (*see also* Ibsen)	*Thanhouser*	(3)(N)

361 HERMAN, Henry

Jan 1908	The Silver King (*see also* Jones)	*Lubin*	(1)(P)

362 HERNE, James A.

Mar 1914	Hearts of Oak	*Mohawk*	(5)(N)
Oct 1914	Shore Acres	*All Star*	(5)(N)

363 HERSCHFIELD, Harry

Nov 1911	Desperate Desmond Almost Succeeds	*Nestor*	(X)(C)
Dec 1911	Desperate Desmond Pursued by Claude Eclair	*Nestor*	(X)(C)
Dec 1911	Desperate Desmond Abducts Rosamund	*Nestor*	(X)(C)
Dec 1911	Desperate Desmond Foiled by Claude Eclair	*Nestor*	(X)(C)
Jan 1912	Desperate Desmond Fails	*Nestor*	(X)(C)
Jan 1912	Desperate Desmond on the Trail Again	*Nestor*	(X)(C)
Feb 1912	Desperate Desmond at the Cannon's Mouth	*Nestor*	(X)(C)

364 HERVEY, William A.

Aug 1915	Aftermath	*Famous Players*	(4)(N)

365 HEWEN, Loring M.

Aug 1914	Treasure Trove	*Edison*	(1)(S)

366 HEWLETT, Maurice Henry

Apr 1915	The Spanish Jade (*see also* Vance)	*Fiction*	(4)(N)

367 HICHENS, Robert Smythe

Oct 1915	Bella Donna *(see also* Fagan*)*	*Famous Players*	(5)(N)

368 HICKS, Sir Seymour

Jan 1915	A Prehistoric Love Story	*Zenith*	(2)(P)

369 HIGGINS, David K.

Oct 1914	His Last Dollar *(see also* Cooke*)*	*Famous Players*	(5)(N)

HILL, Grace Livingston *see* Lutz

370 HILLIARD, Robert

Feb 1915	The Avalanche	*Life Photo*	(5)(N)

371 HOBART, George Vere

Nov 1914	Mrs Black is Back	*Famous Players*	(5)(N)
Jan 1915	Wildfire	*World*	(5)(N)
Oct 1915	The Yankee Girl	*Morosco*	(5)(N)

372 HOFFMAN, Aaron

Nov 1913	Shadows of a Great City *(see also* Blaché*)*	*Hepworth*	(4)(P)
Nov 1915	The Politicians	*Kleine*	(5)(P)

373 HOLLAND, Frank

Oct 1899	Chokee Bill and the Baby	*Riley*	(X)(C)
Oct 1899	Chokee Bill and the Milk	*Riley*	(X)(C)
Oct 1899	Chokee Bill and the Whitewash	*Riley*	(X)(C)

374 HOLMES, Mary Jane

Jul 1910	Tempest and Sunshine	*Thanhouser*	(1)(S)
Aug 1910	Lena Rivers	*Thanhouser*	(1)(N)
Sep 1914	Tempest and Sunshine	*Imp*	(2)(S)
Oct 1914	Lena Rivers	*Garrison*	(5)(N)

375 HOLMES, Oliver Wendell

Dec 1912	The Wonderful One-horse Shay *(The Deacon's Masterpiece; or, The Wonderful 'One-Hoss Shay')*	*Lubin*	(1)(Pm)
Mar 1914	Elsie Venner	*Kennedy*	(3)(N)

376 HOMER

Jan 1911	The Fall of Troy *(The Iliad)*	*Itala*	(1)(Pm)
Feb 1912	The Odyssey	*Milano*	(1)(Pm)

377 HOOD, Thomas

Oct 1908	The Bridge of Sighs	*Edison*	(1)(Pm)
Nov 1908	The Song of the Shirt	*Biograph*	(X)(Pm)

378 HOPE, Anthony (Sir Anthony Hope Hawkins)

Sep 1900	English Nell *(see also* Rose*)*	*Biograph*	(X)(S)
Feb 1913	The Prisoner of Zenda	*Famous Players*	(4)(N)
Mar 1914	The Prisoner of Zenda *(see also* Rose*)*	*London*	(5)(N)
Mar 1914	Rupert of Hentzau	*London*	(5)(N)

379 HOPWOOD, Avery

Mar 1914	Clothes *(see also* Pollock*)*	*Famous Players*	(4)(N)
Aug 1915	Judy Forgot	*Universal*	(5)(N)

380 HORAN, Charles

Aug 1914	When a Woman Loves	*Rolfe*	(5)(N)

381 HORNBLOW, Arthur

May 1915	The Profligate	*Essanay*	(3)(N)
Jul 1915	Kindling	*Lasky*	(5)(N)
	(*see also* Kenyon)		

382 HORNUNG, Ernest William

Aug 1905	Raffles the Amateur Cracksman	*Vitagraph*	(X)(S)
Dec 1905	The Society Raffles	*Biograph*	(X)(S)
Jan 1909	Raffles Escapes from Prison	*Nordisk*	(X)(S)
Apr 1910	Raffles the Amateur Burglar	*Gaumont*	(X)(S)
Jun 1911	Raffles the Gentleman Thief	*New Agency*	(1)(S)
Nov 1915	Stingaree	*Kalem*	(serial)(N)

383 HOSKEN, Heath

Jul 1913	Zoe, a Woman's Last Card	*Hecla*	(N)
	(*see also* Stanton)		

384 HOUSTON, Margaret Belle

Mar 1915	The Little Straw Wife	*Essanay*	(3)(S)

385 HOWARD, George Bronson

Feb 1913	Shenandoah	*Kalem*	(3)(N)
Apr 1914	The Banker's Daughter	*Life Photo*	(5)(N)
Jun 1914	One of our Girls	*Famous Players*	(4)(N)
Jul 1914	The Oubliette	*Bison*	(3)(N)
Jul 1914	The Higher Law	*Bison*	(2)(N)
Aug 1914	Ninety Black Boxes	*Universal*	(3)(N)
Nov 1914	Aristocracy	*Famous Players*	(4)(N)
Dec 1914	Young Mrs Winthrop	*Edison*	(2)(N)
Jan 1915	The Quality of Mercy	*Vitagraph*	(4)(N)
Apr 1915	Snobs	*Lasky*	(5)(N)
Sep 1915	An Enemy to Society	*Metro*	(5)(N)

386 HOWARD, Walter

Mar 1915	The Midnight Wedding	*B & C*	(4)(P)

387 HOWE, Julia Ward

Jun 1911	The Battle Hymn of the Republic	*Vitagraph*	(1)(Sg)

388 HOYT, Charles Hale

1894	A Milk-white Flag	*Edison*	(X)(P)
May 1915	A Midnight Bell	*Selig*	(2)(P)
Jul 1915	A Texas Steer	*Selig*	(3)(P)
Aug 1915	A Bunch of Keys	*Essanay*	(4)(P)
Sep 1915	The Black Sheep	*Selig*	(5)(P)

389 HUDSON, Eric

Aug 1914	Man's Enemy	*Klaw & Erlanger*	(3)(P)

390 HUGHES, Rupert

Jun 1914	Nina of the Theatre	*Kalem*	(2)(S)
Jun 1914	His Wife and His Work	*Vitagraph*	(1)(S)
Nov 1914	The Man That Might Have Been	*Vitagraph*	(1)(S)
Apr 1915	Out of the Ruins *(Miss 318 and Mr 37)*	*Edison*	(4)(N)
Jul 1915	All for a Girl	*Mirrorgraph*	(4)(N)
Sep 1915	The Bigger Man *(The Bridge)*	*Rolfe*	(5)(N)
Nov 1915	The Danger Signal *(Canavan, the Man Who Had His Way)*	*Kleine*	(5)(N)
Dec 1915	Excuse Me	*Pathé*	(5)(N)
Dec 1915	What Will People Say?	*Popular*	(5)(N)

391 HUGO, Victor-Marie

Oct 1905	Esméralda *(Notre-Dame de Paris)*	*Gaumont*	(X)(N)
Nov 1905	The Ex-Convict *(Les Misérables)*	*Pathé*	(X)(N)
Nov 1907	Angelo, Tyrant of Padua	*Nordisk*	(1)(P)
Jan 1909	Ruy Blas	*Vitagraph*	(1)(P)
Mar 1909	A Fool's Revenge *(Le Roi s'amuse)* *(see also* Verdi*)*	*Biograph*	(1)(P)

Jun 1909	Francis I and the Jester's Daughter *(Le Roi s'amuse)*	*SCAGL*	(1)(P)
Jun 1909	The Duke's Jester *(Le Roi s'amuse)(see also* Verdi*)*	*Vitagraph*	(1)(P)
Aug 1909	The Price of a Soul *(Les Misérables)*	*Edison*	(X)(N)
Sep 1909	The Ordeal *(Les Misérables)*	*Edison*	(1)(N)
Sep 1909	The Galley Slave *(Les Misérables)*	*Vitagraph*	(1)(N)
Sep 1909	Fantine, or a Mother's Love *(Les Misérables)*	*Vitagraph*	(1)(N)
Sep 1909	Cosette *(Les Misérables)*	*Vitagraph*	(1)(N)
Sep 1909	Jean Valjean *(Les Misérables)*	*Vitagraph*	(1)(N)
Oct 1909	A New Life *(Les Misérables)*	*Edison*	(1)(N)
1910	Marie Stuart	*SCAGL*	(1)(S)
1910	Hernani	*SCAGL*	(1)(P)
1911	Le Roi s'amuse	*SCAGL*	(1)(P)
1911	Notre-Dame de Paris	*SCAGL*	(1)(N)
1911	Cromwell	*SCAGL*	(1)(P)
Jan 1912	Ruy Blas	*Pathé*	(2)(P)
1912	Marie Tudor	*SCAGL*	(1)(P)
1912	Les Misérables	*SCAGL*	(2)(N)
Feb 1913	Lucretia Borgia *(Lucrèce Borgia)*	*Eclectic*	(4)(P)
Feb 1913	Notre Dame *(Notre-Dame de Paris)*	*Pathé*	(2)(N)
Apr 1913	Les Misérables	*Eclectic*	(9)(N)
Apr 1913	The Bishop's Candlesticks *(Les Misérables)*	*Imp*	(2)(N)
Feb 1914	Ruy Blas	*Majestic*	(3)(P)
1914	Quatre-Vingt-Treize	*SCAGL*	(3)(N)

392 HUME, Fergus (Ferguson Wright Hume)

Sep 1915	The Mystery of a Hansom Cab	*B & C*	(5)(N)

HUMPHREYS, Eliza Margaret *see* Rita

393 HUMPHREYS, Joseph

Oct 1914 The Ragged Earl *Popular* (4)(P)
(*see also* Donnelly; Lacey)

394 HUNT, Leigh

Sep 1907 Francesca Da Rimini *Vitagraph* (X)(Pm)
(*The Story of Rimini*)

Jul 1910 Francesca Da Rimini *Pathé* (1)(Pm)
(*The Story of Rimini*)

395 HURLBUT, William James

Jul 1915 The Fighting Hope *Lasky* (5)(N)

Sep 1915 Body and Soul *Frohman* (5)(N)

396 HYMER, John B.

Oct 1914 The Path Forbidden *Excelsior* (5)(N)

Nov 1914 When Fate Leads Trump *Excelsior* (5)(N)
(*see also* Roberts, Alice M.)

Jan 1915 In the Shadows *Excelsior* (5)(N)

397 IBÁÑEZ, Vicente Blasco

1915 Debout Les Morts *Film d'Art* (5)(N)
(*The Four Horsemen of the Apocalypse*)

IBBOT, Arthur Pearson *see* Bertram, Arthur

398 IBSEN, Henrik

Apr 1911 Pillars of Society *Thanhouser* (1)(P)

Jul 1911 A Doll's House *Thanhouser* (1)(P)

Dec 1911	The Lady from the Sea	*Thanhouser*	(1)(P)
Dec 1911	Sins of the Father *(Ghosts)*	*Lubin*	(1)(P)
Jun 1913	King René's Daughter (*see also* Heri)	*Thanhouser*	(3)(P)
May 1915	Ghosts	*Reliance*	(5)(P)
Sep 1915	Peer Gynt	*Morosco*	(5)(P)

399 ILLICA, Luigi

Jul 1914	Germania	*Savoia*	(5)(N)

400 INGOLDSBY, Thomas

Nov 1913	The Little Vulgar Boy	*Clarendon*	(1)(Pm)

401 INGRAM, Eleanor M.

Aug 1913	The Stolen Woman	*Reliance*	(2)(N)
Apr 1915	The Unafraid	*Lasky*	(5)(N)

402 IRVING, Washington

Oct 1896	Rip Van Winkle	*Biograph*	(X)(S)
Apr 1903	Rip Van Winkle	*Lubin*	(X)(S)
May 1903	Rip Van Winkle	*Biograph*	(X)(S)
Jul 1902	Rip Van Winkle	*Gaumont*	(X)(S)
Jul 1905	Rip Van Winkle	*Méliès*	(1)(S)
Apr 1908	The Legend of Sleepy Hollow	*Kalem*	(1)(S)
May 1908	Rip Van Winkle	*Selig*	(1)(S)
Jul 1910	Columbia	*Thanhouser*	(1)(S)
Aug 1910	Rip Van Winkle	*Thanhouser*	(1)(S)
Sep 1910	Rip Van Winkle	*Columbia*	(1)(S)
Apr 1912	The Legend of Sleepy Hollow	*Éclair*	(1)(S)
Jun 1912	Rip Van Winkle	*Éclair*	(1)(S)
Jun 1912	Rip Van Winkle	*Reliance*	(2)(S)
Jul 1912	Rip Van Winkle	*Vitagraph*	(2)(S)
Nov 1912	Rip Van Winkle	*Union*	(2)(S)
Dec 1912	John Colter's Escape *(Astoria)*	*Selig*	(1)(S)
Jan 1913	The Spectre Bridegroom	*Éclair*	(2)(S)

Feb 1914	Rip Van Winkle *(see also* Boucicault; Storey*)*	*Climax*	(3)(S)
Oct 1914	A Modern Rip Van Winkle *(Rip Van Winkle)*	*American*	(2)(S)
Nov 1914	Rip Van Winkle	*Alco*	(4)(S)
Dec 1914	Rip Van Winkle	*Rolfe*	(4)(S)
Oct 1915	Rip Van Winkle Badly Ripped *(Rip Van Winkle)*	*Novelty*	(1)(S)

403 IRWIN, Will

Apr 1914	Beating Back *(see also* Jennings*)*	*Thanhouser*	(2)(N)

404 ISHAM, Frederic Stewart

Jun 1913	Half a Chance	*Reliance*	(2)(N)

405 IVERS, Julia Crawford

Jul 1915	The Rugmaker's Daughter	*Bosworth*	(4)(N)
Sep 1915	The Majesty of the Law	*Bosworth*	(5)(N)
Oct 1915	Fatherhood	*Bosworth*	(4)(N)

406 JACKSON, Frederick

Sep 1912	A Detective's Strategy *(Thistledown)*	*Selig*	(1)(S)
Feb 1915	Her Martyrdom	*Lubin*	(4)(N)

407 JACKSON, Helen Hunt

May 1910	Ramona	*Biograph*	(1)(N)

408 JACOBS, William Wymark

Feb 1914	Beauty and the Barge	*London*	(1)(S)
Feb 1914	Lawyer Quince	*London*	(1)(S)
Feb 1914	The Bosun's Mate	*London*	(1)(S)
Feb 1914	The Third String	*London*	(1)(S)

Feb 1915	The Monkey's Paw	*Magnet*	(3)(P)
Dec 1915	His Lordship	*London*	(2)(S)
Dec 1915	Her Uncle	*London*	(1)(S)

409 JAMES, Edgar

Jul 1915	Master of the House	*Cosmo*	(5)(N)
Oct 1915	Not Guilty *(Justice)*	*Triumph*	(5)(N)

410 JAMES, Gertrude De S. Wentworth

May 1915	The Devil's Profession	*Arrow*	(3)(N)

JANVIER, F. De H. *see* De Janvier

411 JAY, Harriet

Jun 1915	Alone in London *(see also* Buchanan, Robert*)*	*Turner*	(4)(N)

412 JENNINGS, Al

Apr 1914	Beating Back *(see also* Irwin*)*	*Thanhouser*	(6)(N)

413 JEROME, Jerome Klapka

Jan 1915	Hanging a Picture *(Three Men in a Boat)*	*Williams*	(1)(N)

414 JERROLD, Douglas

May 1908	Black-eyed Susan	*Gaumont*	(X)(P)
Jan 1913	Black-eyed Susan	*London*	(1)(P)
May 1914	Black-eyed Susan	*B & C*	(3)(P)

415 JOHN, Eugenie

Dec 1912	Old Mam'selle's Secret	*Reliance*	(2)(S)

416 JOHNSON, Owen

Dec 1915	The Salamander	*Moss*	(5)(N)

417 JOHNSTONE, Calder

Jan 1914	The Militant	*Imp*	(3)(S)
Feb 1915	The Recoil	*Universal*	(2)(S)
Jun 1915	The Tinker of Stubbinville	*Universal*	(2)(S)
Jul 1915	The Honor of Kenneth McGrath	*Powers*	(2)(S)

418 JOKAI, Maurus

Nov 1915	The Hungarian Nabob	*Biograph*	(4)(N)

419 JONES, Henry Arthur

Jan 1908	The Silver King (*see also* Herman)	*Lubin*	(1)(P)
Feb 1913	The Evangelist	*Lubin*	(4)(P)
Dec 1913	Hoodman Blind	*Pilot*	(4)(P)
Jan 1915	The Dancing Girl	*Famous Players*	(5)(P)
Feb 1915	The Middleman	*London*	(5)(P)
Nov 1915	The Masqueraders	*Famous Players*	(5)(P)
Dec 1915	Lydia Gilmore	*Famous Players*	(5)(P)

420 KAMM, S. J.

Mar 1914	David Gray's Estate	*American*	(1)(S)

421 KAUFMANN, Reginald W.

Aug 1913	The House of Bondage	*Kaybee*	(3)(N)

422 KEENE, Herbert

Oct 1896	The Broken Melody (*see also* Tanner)	*Collings*	(X)(P)

423 KELLAND, Clarence Budington

Sep 1914	The Investment *(You Never Can Tell)*	*Lubin*	(1)(S)

424 KENNEDY, Charles Rann

1915	The Servant in the House	*Selig*	(5)(P)

425 KENYON, Charles A.

Jan 1915	Mignon *(see also* Goethe*)*	*California*	(5)(N)

426 KESTER, Paul

Oct 1915	Angelo Lee	*Vitagraph*	(3)(S)
Nov 1915	The Gypsy Trail *(Gone to the Dogs)*	*Vitagraph*	(2)(S)

427 KEY, Francis Scott

Aug 1910	From Tyranny to Liberty	*Edison*	(1)(S)

428 KIDDER, Edward E.

Jul 1914	Shannon of the Sixth	*Selig*	(5)(N)
Dec 1915	Life's Pitfalls	*Edison*	(3)(N)

429 KILDARE, Owen

Oct 1915	Regeneration *(see also* Hackett*)*	*Fox*	(5)(N)

430 KING, Basil

Jun 1915	The Wild Olive *(see also* Harris, Elmer Blaney; Morosco*)*	*Morosco*	(5)(N)

431 KINGSLEY, Charles

Nov 1907	The Water-babies	*Clarendon*	(1)(N)
May 1910	The Unchanging Sea *(The Three Fishers)*	*Biograph*	(1)(Pm)
Jul 1912	The Sands of Dee	*Biograph*	(1)(Pm)

432 KINKEAD, Eleanor Talbot

Jan 1913	The House in the Woods	*Lubin*	(1)(S)
Jun 1913	The Rose of May	*Selig*	(1)(S)
May 1914	The Lost Sermon	*American*	(1)(S)
Oct 1914	Rosemary, That's for Remembrance	*Selig*	(1)(S)
Mar 1915	The Wood Nymph	*Essanay*	(2)(S)

433 KINSELLA, Frank

Oct 1915	Bred in the Bone	*Reliance*	(4)(N)

434 KIPLING, (Joseph) Rudyard

Sep 1910	The Vampire	*Selig*	(1)(Pm)
May 1911	Gunga Din	*Powers*	(1)(Pm)
May 1911	Soldiers Three	*Vitagraph*	(1)(S)
Apr 1913	The Vampire of the Desert *(The Vampire)*	*Vitagraph*	(2)(Pm)
May 1913	The Fool *(The Vampire)*	*Big Ben*	(3)(Pm)
Aug 1913	A Maid of Mandalay *(Mandalay)*	*Vitagraph*	(1)(Pm)
Jan 1915	A Fool There Was *(The Vampire)(see also* Browne, Porter Emerson*)*	*Fox*	(5)(Pm)
Mar 1915	The City of Terrible Night *(The City of Dreadful Night)*	*Imp*	(2)(S)

435 KISTEMAECKERS, Henry Hubert Alexandre

1914	Instinct	*Film d'Art*	(2)(S)
1915	La Flambée	*Film d'Art*	(2)(S)

436 KLEIN, Charles

Dec 1913	The Third Degree	*Lubin*	(5)(P)
Jan 1914	The Daughters of Men	*Lubin*	(5)(P)
Feb 1914	The Lion and the Mouse	*Lubin*	(5)(P)
Mar 1914	The Gamblers	*Lubin*	(5)(P)

Jan 1915	The District Attorney (*see also* Fiske)	*Lubin*	(5)(P)

437 KNOBLAUCH, Edward

Dec 1914	Kismet	*Zenith*	(4)(P)
Jul 1915	The Shulamite (*see also* Askew)	*London*	(4)(N)

438 KNOWLES, James Sheridan

Jan 1909	Virginius	*Vitagraph*	(1)(P)
May 1912	Virginius	*Reliance*	(1)(P)

439 KOCH, Mae C.

Feb 1915	The Silent Plea	*Vitagraph*	(3)(N)

440 KREMER, Theodore

May 1914	The Fatal Wedding	*Biograph*	(3)(P)

441 KUMMER, Frederic Arnold (Arnold Fredericks)

Dec 1913	The Adventure of the Actress's Jewels	*Edison*	(1)(S)
Feb 1914	The Adventure of the Extra Baby	*Edison*	(1)(S)
Mar 1914	The Adventure of the Alarm Clock	*Edison*	(1)(S)
Apr 1914	The Adventure of the Stolen Slipper	*Edison*	(1)(S)
Apr 1914	The Brute	*Famous Players*	(4)(N)
May 1914	The Adventure of the Counterfeit Money	*Edison*	(1)(S)
Jun 1914	The Adventure of the Missing Legacy	*Edison*	(1)(S)
Sep 1914	The Adventure of the Hasty Elopement	*Edison*	(1)(S)
Oct 1914	The Adventure of the Smuggled Diamonds	*Edison*	(1)(S)
Nov 1914	The Adventure of the Lost Wife	*Edison*	(1)(S)

Dec 1914	The Adventure of the Wrong Santa Claus	*Edison*	(1)(S)
Mar 1915	Mr Buttles	*Essanay*	(3)(N)
Sep 1915	The Ivory Snuffbox	*Brady*	(5)(N)
Nov 1915	One Million Dollars *(One Million Francs)*	*Rolfe*	(5)(N)

442 KYNE, Peter Barnard

Jan 1915	Broncho Billy and the Baby	*Essanay*	(1)(S)
Aug 1915	It Happened While He Fished	*Nestor*	(1)(S)
Sep 1915	Judge Not *(Renunciation)*	*Universal*	(1)(S)
Oct 1915	The Long Chance	*Universal*	(1)(S)
Nov 1915	What the River Foretold	*Bison*	(1)(S)

443 LACEY, Ernest

Oct 1914	The Ragged Earl *(see also* Donnelly; Humphreys*)*	*Popular*	(4)(N)

444 LA FONTAINE, Jean de

Jul 1908	The Miller, His Son and His Donkey	*Pathé*	(X)(Pm)
Mar 1910	A Light Heart Is Better Than Riches	*Pathé*	(1)(Pm)
Jun 1910	The Miller, His Son and His Donkey	*Pathé*	(1)(Pm)
Apr 1910	The Grasshopper and the Ant	*Pathé*	(1)(Pm)
Jan 1911	The Cobbler and the Financier	*Pathé*	(1)(Pm)
1911	La Cigale	*Eclipse*	(1)(Pm)
May 1912	Henry IV and the Woodchopper	*SCAGL*	(1)(Pm)
Jan 1913	The Cobbler and the Financier	*Pathé*	(1)(Pm)
Aug 1913	La Cigale	*Close*	(2)(Pm)

445 LAIT, Jack

Apr 1915	Help Wanted	*Bosworth*	(4)(N)

446 LAKE, Lew

Oct 1912 The Bloomsbury Burglars *Cinema Prods.* (2)(P)

447 LANDECK, Benjamin

Nov 1908 Saved from the Sea *Gaumont* (1)(P)
(*see also* Shirley)
Apr 1910 Tommy Atkins *Gaumont* (1)(P)
(*see also* Shirley)
Jan 1915 Tommy Atkins *Barker* (4)(P)
(*see also* Shirley)
Sep 1915 Jack Tar *Barker* (5)(P)
(*see also* Shirley)
Dec 1915 The Two Roads *London* (4)(P)

448 LANGDON, Charles B.

Jul 1914 Man's Enemy *Biograph* (4)(N)

449 LARDNER, Ring (Ringgold Wilmer Lardner)

Jul 1915 Letters from Bugs to Gus *World* (1)(S)

450 LASHELLE, Kirke

Oct 1913 Checkers *All Star* (6)(P)
(*see also* Blossom)
Sep 1914 The Virginian *Lasky* (5)(P)
(*see also* Wister)

451 LAW, Arthur

Nov 1914 The Country Mouse *Bosworth* (4)(N)

452 LAWRENCE, Wood

May 1915 Mizpah, or Love's Sacrifice *Magnet* (4)(P)

453 LAWSON, John

Sep 1913	Humanity, or Only a Jew	*Barker*	(3)(P)

454 LAWSON, Wilbur

Sep 1915	The Wonderful Adventure	*Fox*	(6)(N)

455 LEBLANC, Maurice

Jun 1910	Arsène Lupin	*Vitaskop*	(1)(N)
Sep 1910	The Blue Diamond	*Vitaskop*	(1)(S)
Dec 1910	The Two Rembrandts	*Vitaskop*	(1)(S)
Jul 1914	Lupin the Gentleman Burglar *(Arsène Lupin, Gentleman Cambrioleur)*	*Pasquali*	(3)(N)
Apr 1915	The Gentleman Burglar *(Arsène Lupin)*	*Selig*	(2)(N)

456 LEFANU, Joseph Sheridan

Dec 1905	Shamus O'Brien	*Cricks*	(X)(Pm)
Mar 1908	Shamus O'Brien	*Selig*	(1)(Pm)
Mar 1912	Shamus O'Brien	*Imp*	(2)(Pm)

457 LEGOUVÉ, Ernest Wilfred

1912	Adrienne Lecouvreur *(see also* Sardou; Scribe*)*	*Film d'Art*	(2)(P)

458 LEHÁR, Franz (Ferencz Lehár)

Sep 1907	The Merry Widow *(Die Lustige Witwe)*	*Nordisk*	(X)(O)
Dec 1907	The Merry Widow *(Die Lustige Witwe)*	*Kalem*	(1)(O)

459 LEIGHTON, Robert

May 1904	Convict 99 *(see also* Connor*)*	*Gaumont*	(1)(N)

460 LEMAÎTRE, Jules

Apr 1908	The Return of Ulysses	*Film D'Art*	(X)(P)

461 LENGYEL, Maynhardt

Oct 1914	Typhoon	*Paramount*	(4)(N)

462 LEONARD, Herbert

Jul 1915	The Girl of My Heart	*British Empire*	(5)(P)

463 LEONCAVALLO, Ruggiero

1907	I Pagliacci	*Ambrosio*	(1)(O)
Feb 1909	I Pagliacci	*Lubin*	(1)(O)

LE PRINCE DE BEAUMONT, Madame *see* **De Beaumont**

464 LE QUEUX, William

Oct 1914	If England Were Invaded *(The Invasion of 1910)*	*Gaumont*	(2)(N)
Jun 1915	Sons of Satan	*London*	(5)(N)
Dec 1915	No Greater Love	*Selig*	(4)(N)

465 LEROUX, Gaston

1913	The Mystery of the Yellow Room	*Éclair*	(3)(N)
Jan 1913	Balaoo	*Éclair*	(4)(N)
1913	Cheri-Bibi	*Éclair*	(4)(N)
May 1914	Larsan's Last Incarnation *(The Perfume of the Lady in Black)*	*Éclair*	(4)(N)
1915	Alsace	*Film d'Art*	(4)(N)

466 LESSING, Bruno (Rudolph Block)

Apr 1915	The Faith of Her Fathers *(A Daughter of Israel)*	*Universal*	(3)(N)

Jul 1915	A Hunchback's Romance	*Imp*	(2)(S)
Sep 1915	When the Call Came *(The Song of Songs)*	*Imp*	(2)(S)

467 LESTOCQ, W. H.

Dec 1915	Jane *(see also* Nicholls*)*	*Morosco*	(5)(P)

468 LEVY, José G.

May 1915	A Daughter of England *(see also* Miller, E.V.*)*	*British Empire*	(4)(P)

469 LIDELL, H.

Nov 1913	Jerry's Mother-in-Law *(see also* Brown*)*	*Vitagraph*	(3)(S)

470 LIEBE, Hapsburg

Sep 1912	Circumstantial Evidence *(The Little Good)*	*Selig*	(1)(S)

471 LILLIBRIDGE, W.

Oct 1914	Where the Trail Divides	*Lasky*	(5)(N)

472 LILLO, George

Feb 1913	George Barnwell, the London Apprentice *(The History of George Barnwell)*	*Hepworth*	(2)(P)

473 LINCOLN, Abraham

Jun 1912	Lincoln's Gettysburg Address	*Vitagraph*	(1)(NF)

474 LINCOLN, Joseph Crosby

Mar 1913	Tea and Toast *(The Postmaster)*	*Edison*	(1)(S)
1915	Partners of the Tide	*Eastern*	(5)(N)

475 LINDO, Frank

Sep 1915	Home *(Home, Sweet Home)*	*B & C*	(4)(P)

476 LINDSAY, Mary (Lady Anne Barnard)

Oct 1910	Auld Robin Gray	*Vitagraph*	(1)(Pm)

477 LLEWELLYN, Fewlass

Jul 1915	The Coal King *(see also* Martin*)*	*Neptune*	(4)(P)

478 LLOYD, John

Aug 1913	The Invaders	*Kalem*	(2)(S)

479 LOCKE, D. R.

Oct 1914	The Senator's Lady *(Hannah Jane)*	*Powers*	(1)(S)

480 LOCKE, Edward

Sep 1915	The Case of Becky	*Lasky*	(5)(N)

481 LOCKE, William John

Jan 1915	The Glory of Clementina	*Edison*	(5)(N)
Jan 1915	The Morals of Marcus *(The Morals of Marcus Ordeyne)*	*Famous Players*	(5)(N)
Jun 1915	The Beloved Vagabond	*Pathé*	(5)(N)

Sep 1915	Simon the Jester	*Pathé*	(5)(N)

482 LOMAX, Fawcett

May 1915	The Wrong Woman	*Edison*	(3)(N)

483 LONDON, Jack

Aug 1907	The Sea-Wolf's Finish *(The Sea-Wolf)*	*Kalem*	(X)(N)
Aug 1908	For the Love of Gold *(Just Meat)*	*Biograph*	(1)(N)
Oct 1908	The Call of the Wild	*Biograph*	(1)(N)
Oct 1913	The Sea-Wolf	*Balboa*	(4)(N)
Oct 1913	The Sea-Wolf	*Bosworth*	(7)(N)
Dec 1913	A Piece of Steak *(When God Laughs)*	*Balboa*	(4)(N)
Dec 1913	To Kill a Man *(The Night Born)*	*Balboa*	(4)(N)
Jul 1914	John Barleycorn	*Bosworth*	(5)(N)
Jul 1914	Martin Eden	*Bosworth*	(5)(N)
Jul 1914	The Sands of Life	*Balboa*	(2)(S)
Aug 1914	The Call of the Wild	*Famous Players*	(5)(N)
Aug 1914	An Odyssey of the North	*Bosworth*	(5)(N)
Aug 1914	The Valley of the Moon	*Bosworth*	(6)(N)
Dec 1914	Burning Daylight	*Bosworth*	(5)(N)
Feb 1915	It's No Laughing Matter	*Bosworth*	(5)(N)

484 LONG, Dillon

Oct 1914	In the Glare of the Lights	*Essanay*	(3)(S)

485 LONG, John Luther

Dec 1910	The Captain's Bride *(The Baby Grand)*	*Edison*	(1)(S)
Jul 1915	The Fox Woman	*Majestic*	(4)(N)
Oct 1915	Madame Butterfly *(see also* Belasco)	*Famous Players*	(5)(N)

486 LONGFELLOW, Henry Wadsworth

Sep 1897	The Village Blacksmith	*Paul*	(X)(Pm)
Sep 1903	Hiawatha	*Urban*	(1)(Pm)
Nov 1905	The Village Blacksmith	*Clarendon*	(X)(Pm)
Sep 1907	The Courtship of Miles Standish	*Kalem*	(1)(Pm)
Feb 1908	Evangeline	*Kalem*	(1)(Pm)
Nov 1908	The Village Blacksmith	*Cricks*	(X)(Pm)
Sep 1909	Hiawatha	*Imp*	(1)(Pm)
Jan 1910	The Courtship of Miles Standish	*Selig*	(1)(Pm)
Mar 1910	The Death of Minnehaha *(Hiawatha)*	*Imp*	(1)(Pm)
Dec 1911	Evangeline	*Selig*	(1)(Pm)
Sep 1912	The Old Clock on the Stairs	*Éclair*	(1)(Pm)
Jun 1912	The Vision Beautiful *(The Legend Beautiful)*	*Selig*	(1)(Pm)
Nov 1912	King Robert of Sicily	*Hepworth*	(1)(Pm)
Jan 1913	The Village Blacksmith	*Lubin*	(1)(Pm)
Feb 1913	The Flaming Forge *(The Village Blacksmith)*	*Selig*	(1)(Pm)
Feb 1913	Hiawatha	*Moore*	(4)(Pm)
Jul 1913	His Mother's Birthday	*Imp*	(1)(Pm)
Jul 1913	Hiawatha	*Kinemacolor*	(2)(Pm)
Aug 1913	The Village Blacksmith	*Powers*	(1)(Pm)
Aug 1913	King Robert of Sicily	*Essanay*	(3)(Pm)
Nov 1913	The Children's Hour	*Thanhouser*	(1)(Pm)
Nov 1913	Evangeline	*Canadian Bioscope*	(4)(Pm)
Oct 1914	The Midnight Ride of Paul Revere	*Edison*	(2)(Pm)
Aug 1915	The Little Boy Who Once Was He	*Reliance*	(1)(Pm)

487 LORIMER, Wright

1915	The Shepherd King	*Broadway*	(5)(N)

488 LOVER, Samuel

Oct 1911	Rory O'More	*Kalem*	(1)(Pm)

489 LUTHER, Mark Lee

Dec 1914	The Crucible	*Famous Players*	(5)(N)

490 LUTZ, Grace (Grace Livingston Hill)

Nov 1914	The Best Man	*Edison*	(1)(S)
Jul 1915	The Mystery of Mary	*Vitagraph*	(3)(N)

491 LYNDE, Francis

Jul 1914	Across the Burning Trestle *(In Christmas Canyon)*	*Edison*	(1)(S)

492 LYON, Gertrude

Nov 1914	What Could She Do?	*Edison*	(2)(S)
Mar 1915	On the Stroke of Twelve	*Edison*	(3)(S)
Jun 1915	Through Turbulent Waters	*Edison*	(4)(S)

493 LYTTON, Edward George Earle Lytton Bulwer-

Jul 1900	The Last Days of Pompeii	*Paul*	(X)(N)
1908	Damon and Pythias	*Selig*	(X)(S)
Dec 1908	The Last Days of Pompeii	*Ambrosio*	(1)(N)
Apr 1909	The Last Days of Pompeii	*Raleigh*	(1)(N)
Dec 1909	The Christian Martyrs *(The Last Days of Pompeii)*	*Selig*	(1)(N)
Dec 1909	Richelieu *(see also* Booth*)*	*Vitagraph*	(1)(P)
Feb 1910	The Roman	*Selig*	(1)(N)
Jan 1911	Justinian and Theodora	*Selig*	(1)(S)
Jun 1911	The Cardinal's Edict *(Richelieu)*	*Edison*	(1)(P)
Jun 1913	The Last Days of Pompeii	*Pasquali*	(4)(N)
Jun 1913	The Last Days of Pompeii	*Ambrosio*	(4)(N)
Jun 1913	Eugene Aram	*Cricks*	(4)(N)
Oct 1913	The Lady of Lyons	*Hepworth*	(4)(P)

Nov 1913	The End of the Road *(Eugene Aram)*	*Gem*	(2)(N)
May 1914	Cardinal Richelieu's Ward *(Richelieu)*	*Thanhouser*	(6)(P)
Sep 1914	Richelieu	*Bison*	(4)(P)
Nov 1914	Ernest Maltravers	*Biograph*	(2)(N)
Dec 1914	Damon and Pythias	*Universal*	(6)(N)
Jan 1915	Night and Morning	*Clarendon*	(3)(N)
Jan 1915	Money	*Biograph*	(2)(P)
Jul 1915	Eugene Aram	*Edison*	(5)(N)

494 McCLELLAN, Charles M. S.

Nov 1913	Leah Kleschna	*Famous Players*	(5)(P)

495 McCULLOUGH, Campbell

May 1913	Kelly from the Emerald Isle *(see also* Gillmore*)*	*Solax*	(3)(P)

496 McCUTCHEON, George Barr

Apr 1914	Brewster's Millions *(see also* Smith, Winchell; Stone*)*	*Lasky*	(5)(N)
Aug 1914	Beverly of Graustark	*Klaw & Erlanger*	(5)(N)
Oct 1914	What's His Name	*Lasky*	(5)(N)
Nov 1914	The Circus Man *(The Rose and the Ring)*	*Lasky*	(5)(N)
Apr 1915	Graustark *(Beverly of Graustark)*	*Essanay*	(5)(N)
Nov 1915	Nedra	*Pathé*	(5)(N)

497 MacDONALD, Ronald

Jun 1915	Gambler's Advocate	*Famous Players*	(4)(P)

498 McELVRAY, Robert C.

Aug 1915	The Big Brother	*Alliance*	(5)(N)

499 McEVOY, Charles

Mar 1915	The Man in the Attic	*London*	(4)(P)
Aug 1915	The Third Generation	*London*	(5)(N)
Dec 1915	The Man in the Shadows *(Village Wedding)*	*McEvoy*	(3)(S)

500 MacGRATH, Harold

Jul 1914	The Man on the Box	*Lasky*	(5)(N)
Jan 1915	The Goose Girl	*Lasky*	(5)(N)
Jan 1915	The Carpet from Bagdad	*Selig*	(5)(N)
May 1915	The Lure of the Mask	*American*	(5)(N)
Jul 1915	The Puppet Crown *(see also* De Mille, William Churchill*)*	*Lasky*	(5)(N)
Oct 1915	The Voice in the Fog	*Lasky*	(5)(N)
Sep 1914	Hearts and Masks	*Selig*	(3)(N)
Sep 1914	The Rajah's Vacation	*Selig*	(1)(S)

501 MacHUGH, Augustin

Dec 1914	Officer 666	*Kleine*	(6)(N)

502 McINTYRE, John T.

Oct 1915	An Affair of Three Nations	*Pathé*	(5)(N)
Nov 1915	The Menace of the Mute	*Pathé*	(5)(N)
Dec 1915	The House of Fear	*Pathé*	(5)(N)

MACKAY, Marie *see* Corelli

503 MACKAY, W. Gayer

Feb 1915	The King's Outcast *(see also* Ord*)*	*London*	(4)(N)

504 MACKAYE, Steele

Nov 1912	Hazel Kirke	*Majestic*	(2)(P)
Feb 1915	In Spite of All	*Edison*	(3)(P)

505 McNALLY, John J.

1896	The May Irwin–John C. Rice Kiss *(The Widow Jones)*	*Edison*	(X)(P)

506 MacPHERSON, Jean Du Rocher

Sep 1915	Evidence	*Shubert*	(5)(N)

507 MAETERLINCK, Maurice

Feb 1910	The Blue Bird	*Gaumont*	(1)(P)
May 1913	Pelléas and Mélisande	*Bison*	(3)(P)
Feb 1914	Mary Magdalene	*Kennedy*	(3)(P)

508 MAJOR, Charles

Nov 1915	Sweet Alyssum	*Selig*	(5)(N)

509 MALLORY, J. Albert

1911	The Child and the Tramp *(A Knight of the Road)*	*Edison*	(1)(S)

MANN, Nancy *see* Woodrow

510 MANNERS, John Hartley

Jun 1914	The House Next Door	*Lubin*	(5)(N)

511 MANTELL, Robert

Oct 1914	The Face in the Moonlight	*Brady*	(5)(N)

512 MANZONI, Alessandro

Aug 1913 Betrothed *Ambrosio* (6)(N)
(I Promessi Sposi)

513 MAPES, Victor

Apr 1915 The Curious Conduct of Judge Legarde *Life Photo* (5)(N)

514 MARBURGH, Bertram

Aug 1915 Marrying Money *Shubert* (5)(N)
(see also Pezet*)*

515 MARGUERITTE, Paul and Victor

1910 Chien Et Loup *Éclair* (1)(S)
Feb 1910 In the Mirror *Pathé* (1)(S)

516 MARRIOTT, George Moore

Aug 1912 The Maid of the Alps *Terrier* (1)(P)

517 MARRYAT, Frederick

Jan 1915 Midshipman Easy *B & C* (3)(N)
(Mr Midshipman Easy)

518 MARSTON, Lawrence

May 1915 An Innocent Sinner *Kalem* (3)(N)

519 MARTIN, Ernest

Jul 1915 The Coal King *Neptune* (4)(P)
(see also Llewellyn*)*

520 MARY, Jules

Sep 1909 The Ragamuffin's Holiday *SCAGL* (1)(S)
Jan 1914 A Man's Shadow *Eclectic* (6)(N)

Oct 1915	The Man of Shame *(Roger la Honte)*	*Universal*	(5)(N)

521 MASCAGNI, Pietro

1909	Cavalleria Rusticana	*Éclair*	(1)(O)

522 MASON, Alfred Edward Woodley

Mar 1911	Princess Clementina *(see also* Bancroft*)*	*Barker*	(1)(N)
Jun 1915	The Four Feathers	*Dryeda*	(5)(N)
Dec 1915	Green Stockings	*Vitagraph*	(5)(N)

523 MASON, Edith Huntington

Oct 1914	The Real Agatha	*Essanay*	(2)(S)

524 MASSENET, Jules-Émile-Frédéric

Jan 1910	Manon *(Manon Lescaut)(see also* Prévost*)*	*Pathé*	(1)(O)
Jan 1911	The Atonement of Thaïs *(Thaïs)*	*Gaumont*	(1)(O)
Feb 1914	Manon Lescaut *(see also* Prévost*)*	*Playgoers*	(5)(O)

525 MATTHEWS, Frances Amyar

Jun 1915	Insuring Cutey	*Vitagraph*	(2)(S)
Dec 1915	The Thirteenth Girl *(Where Did Lottie Go?)*	*Vitagraph*	(3)(S)

526 MAUGHAM, William Somerset

Sep 1915	The Explorer	*Lasky*	(5)(N)

MAUPASSANT *see* De Maupassant

527 MAXIM, Hudson

Aug 1915	The Battle Cry of Peace *(Defenseless America)*	*Vitagraph*	(9)(N)

528 MAXWELL, Sir Herbert

Nov 1915	Sixty Years a Queen	*Barker*	(8)(Bio)

529 MAYNE, G. E. R.

Jun 1915	A Garret in Bohemia	*London*	(3)(N)
Dec 1915	The Heart of Sister Anne	*London*	(4)(N)

530 MAYO, Margaret

Nov 1914	Behind the Scenes	*Famous Players*	(5)(N)

531 MECHTOLD, Mary Rider

May 1914	The Mountain Rat	*Reliance*	(4)(N)
Nov 1914	The Temple of Moloch	*Edison*	(1)(S)
Apr 1915	Indiscretion *(The Official Introducer)*	*Lubin*	(1)(S)

532 MELFORD, Mark

Dec 1912	Gretna Green	*Heron*	(X)(P)
Jul 1913	Wanted a Husband	*Brightonia*	(X)(P)
Jul 1913	Flying from Justice	*Brightonia*	(2)(P)
Dec 1913	Only a Wedding	*H & W*	(X)(P)
Jun 1915	Flying from Justice	*Neptune*	(4)(P)

533 MELVILLE, Walter and Frederick

Sep 1913	Ivanhoe *(see also Scott, Sir Walter)*	*Zenith*	(4)(P)

Jun 1915	The Beggar Girl's Wedding	*BEF*	(4)(P)
Sep 1915	The Girl Who Took the Wrong Turning	*BEF*	(4)(P)
Nov 1915	The Shopsoiled Girl	*BEF*	(4)(P)
Dec 1915	A World of Sin	*BEF*	(4)(P)

534 MEREDITH, Hal (Harry Blyth)

Oct 1909	Sexton Blake (*see also* Denton; Graydon)	*Gaumont*	(1)(P)
Dec 1909	The Council of Three	*London*	(1)(Ch)
Aug 1910	Jewel Thieves Run to Earth by Sexton Blake	*Gaumont*	(X)(Ch)
Apr 1912	Sexton Blake V. Baron Kettler	*Humanity*	(X)(Ch)
Jul 1914	The Mystery of the Diamond Belt	*Davidson*	(3)(Ch)
Nov 1914	Britain's Secret Treaty	*Davidson*	(3)(Ch)
Nov 1914	The Kaiser's Spies	*Davidson*	(3)(Ch)
Apr 1915	The Stolen Heirlooms	*Davidson*	(3)(Ch)
Jul 1915	The Great Cheque Fraud	*Davidson*	(3)(Ch)
Sep 1915	The Counterfeiters	*Davidson*	(3)(Ch)
Nov 1915	The Thornton Jewel Mystery	*Davidson*	(3)(Ch)

535 MEREDITH, Owen (Earl of Lytton)

Aug 1912	Lucile	*Thanhouser*	(2)(N)
Oct 1914	All Love Excelling	*Eclectic*	(5)(N)

536 MÉRIMÉE, Prosper

Feb 1909	Torero Song *(Carmen)*	*Lubin*	(X)(Sg)
Aug 1909	Carmen	*Film d'Art*	(1)(S)
May 1910	The Cigarette Maker of Seville *(Carmen)*	*Edison*	(1)(S)
Jul 1910	Carmen	*Cosmopolitan*	(1)(S)
May 1912	Carmen	*Feature*	(2)(S)
Apr 1913	Carmen	*Monopol*	(3)(S)
May 1913	Carmen	*Thanhouser*	(3)(S)
Mar 1914	Colomba	*Biograph*	(3)(S)

Nov 1915	Carmen	*Fox*	(5)(S)
Nov 1915	Carmen	*Lasky*	(5)(S)

537 MERSON, Billy

Aug 1915	Billy's Spanish Love Spasm *(Serenata)*	*Homeland*	(3)(P)

538 MERWIN, Samuel

Oct 1915	Comrade John *(see also* Webster, Henry Kitchell*)*	*Balboa*	(5)(N)

539 MEYERBEER, Giacomo

Feb 1910	Robert the Devil	*Lux*	(1)(O)

540 MEYER-FORSTER, Wilhelm M.

Nov 1915	Old Heidelberg *(Karl Heinrich)*	*Triangle*	(5)(N)

541 MICHAELIS, Sophus

1909	The Marriage of Trionville	*Nordisk*	(1)(S)
Mar 1910	A Wedding During the French Revolution *(A Son of the People)*	*Nordisk*	(1)(N)
1915	The Heart of Lady Alaine *(A Son of the People)*	*Nordisk*	(5)(N)

542 MICHELS, Philip Verrill

Oct 1912	Subterfuge	*Selig*	(X)(S)

543 MICHELSON, Miriam

Sep 1915	In the Bishop's Carriage *(see also* Pollock*)*	*Famous Players*	(5)(P)

544 MIDDLETON, George

Dec 1915 The Siren's Song *Shubert* (5)(N)
(*see also* Westervelt)

545 MILLER, E. V.

May 1915 A Daughter of England *BEF* (3)(P)
(*see also* Levy)

546 MILLER, Irene

Nov 1915 Mrs Cassell's Profession *Barker* (4)(N)

547 MILLER, St Aubyn

Jan 1913 The Golden Chance *London* (1)(S)

MIRABEAU, Marie-Antoinette de Riquetti de *see* Gyp

548 MIRABEAU, Octave

Sep 1915 Business is Business *Universal* (6)(N)

549 MITCHELL, Edmund

Apr 1915 The Lone Star Rush *Climax* (5)(N)

550 MITCHELL, John Ames

Nov 1914 The Pines of Lory *Edison* (2)(S)

551 MIZNER, Wilson (*see also* Armstrong)

Apr 1914 The Greyhound *Life Photo* (5)(P)
Jan 1915 The Deep Purple *Liebler* (5)(P)

552 MOFFETT, Cleveland

Oct 1915	The Money Master *(The Battle)*	*Kleine*	(5)(N)

MOINEAUX, Georges *see* Courteline

553 MOLIÈRE (Jean-Baptiste Poquelin)

1908	Don Juan *(Dom Juan)*	*Pathé*	(X)(P)
Oct 1909	The Affected Young Ladies *(Les Précieuses Ridicules)*	*Pathé*	(1)(P)
Jan 1910	The Miser *(L'Avare)*	*Pathé*	(1)(P)
Dec 1910	The Imposter	*Cosmopolitan*	(1)(P)
Jun 1914	The Mock Doctor	*Éclair*	(2)(P)

554 MOLNAR, Franz (Ferenc)

Sep 1908	The Devil	*Edison*	(1)(P)
Oct 1908	The Devil	*Biograph*	(X)(P)
Dec 1908	He Went to See the Devil Play *(The Devil)*	*Vitagraph*	(1)(P)
Mar 1915	The Devil	*New York*	(5)(P)

555 MONTGOMERY, James

Nov 1914	Ready Money	*Lasky*	(5)(N)

556 MOODY, William Vaughn

Dec 1915	The Great Divide	*Lubin*	(5)(P)

557 MOORE, Carlisle (Carlyle)

Feb 1915	Stop, Thief	*Kleinel*	(5)(N)

558 MOORE, Clement Clarke

Dec 1905	The Night Before Christmas *(A Visit from St. Nicholas)*	*Edison*	(X)(Pm)

559 MOORE, Frederick

Dec 1914	At Dawn	*Majestic*	(2)(S)

560 MOORE, Thomas

Jul 1910	The Loves of the Angels	*New Agency*	(1)(Pm)
Mar 1912	You Remember Ellen	*Kalem*	(1)(Pm)
Sep 1912	Believe Me If All Those Endearing Young Charms	*Edison*	(1)(Pm)

561 MOREAU, Émile

Jun 1909	The Escape of the Count De La Valette	*Pathé*	(1)(P)
1912	Queen Elizabeth	*SCAGL*	(6)(P)

562 MOREAU, Eugène

1910	The Lyons Mail	*Cosmo*	(1)(P)
1911	The Orleans Coach	*Pathé*	(1)(P)
Apr 1915	The True Story of the Lyons Mail *(The Lyons Mail)(see also* Reade*)*	*Samuelson*	(2)(P)

563 MOROSCO, Oliver

Apr 1915	Pretty Mrs Smith *(see also* Harris, Elmer Blaney*)*	*Morosco*	(5)(P)
Jul 1915	The Wild Olive *(see also* Harris, Elmer Blaney; King*)*	*Morosco*	(5)(P)

564 MORRIS, Gouveneur

Apr 1914	The Senator's Brother	*Vitagraph*	(5)(N)

565 MORTON, C. S.

Jun 1914 Miss Raffles *Vitagraph* (1)(S)

566 MORTON, Edward

May 1900 San Toy *Biograph* (X)(P)

567 MORTON, J. Madison

Jan 1913 Box and Cox *Crystal* (2)(P)

568 MORTON, Martha

Feb 1915 The Bachelor's Romance *Famous Players* (5)(N)

MOSENTHAL *see* von Mosenthal

569 MOZART, Wolfgang Amadeus

Dec 1913 The Marriage of Figaro *Ambrosio* (2)(O)

570 MUNDY, Talbot

Jul 1912 For Valor *Edison* (1)(S)

571 MURGER, Henry

1913 La Vie de Bohème *SCAGL* (2)(O)
(Scènes de la Vie Bohème)(see also Puccini*)*

572 MURPHY, G. C. T.

Sep 1914 Little Meg and I *Victor* (1)(S)

573 MURPHY, Joseph

Nov 1912 The Kerry Gow *Kalem* (3)(N)

574 MURRAY, Douglas

Aug 1915	The Imposters	*Brody*	(5)(N)

MUSSET *see* de Musset

575 NANKIVEL, Frank E.

Oct 1912	Uncle Mun and the Minister	*Edison*	(1)(C)
Nov 1912	A Thrilling Rescue by Uncle Mun	*Edison*	(1)(C)

576 NESBIT, Edith

Feb 1913	The Ballad of Splendid Silence	*Williams*	(1)(Pm)

577 NEW, Clarence Herbert

Feb 1914	A Leak in the Foreign Office	*Thanhouser*	(2)(S)
Mar 1914	The Cat's Paw	*Thanhouser*	(2)(S)
Apr 1914	A Debut in the Secret Service	*Thanhouser*	(2)(S)

578 NICHOLLS, Harry

Nov 1915	Jane	*Morosco*	(5)(N)
	(see also Lestocq*)*		

579 NICHOLSON, Meredith

Apr 1915	The Port of Missing Men	*Famous Players*	(5)(N)
Aug 1915	The House of a Thousand Candles	*Selig*	(5)(N)
Aug 1915	The Girl with the Red Feather	*Selig*	(5)(N)
Dec 1915	London's Legacy	*Universal*	(5)(N)

580 NORRIS, Frank

Dec 1909	A Corner in Wheat	*Biograph*	(1)(N)
	(The Pit)		
Mar 1914	Desert Gold	*Kaybee*	(2)(N)
	(McTeague)		

Jan 1915	The Pit	*Brady*	(5)(N)
Jul 1915	The Octopus	*Selig*	(3)(N)
	(see also Davis, Charles Belmont*)*		

581 NORTON, Roy

Mar 1910	His First Valentine	*Edison*	(X)(S)
Apr 1910	Sandy the Substitute	*Edison*	(1)(S)
Aug 1910	His New Family	*Edison*	(1)(S)
Sep 1910	The Great Secret	*Edison*	(1)(S)
Oct 1910	The Breach of Discipline	*Edison*	(1)(S)
Nov 1910	The Adoption	*Edison*	(1)(S)
Mar 1911	Between Two Fires	*Edison*	(1)(S)
Aug 1911	The Venom of the Poppy	*Edison*	(1)(S)
Nov 1911	Love and Hatred	*Edison*	(1)(S)
	(The Greater Hate)		
Jul 1915	The Plunderer	*Fox*	(5)(N)
	(see also White, Grace Miller*)*		
Jul 1915	Coincidence	*Biograph*	(5)(N)
Aug 1915	Mister Paganini	*Biograph*	(5)(N)
Sep 1915	And by These Deeds	*Biograph*	(5)(N)
Nov 1915	Packer Jim's Guardianship	*Biograph*	(5)(N)
Dec 1915	The Masterful Hireling	*Biograph*	(5)(N)

582 O'CONNOR, Mary H.

Dec 1912	The Little Turncoat	*Kaybee*	(2)(S)
1913	A Southern Cinderella	*Domino*	(1)(S)
	(Soul of the South)		
Dec 1913	Sacrifice	*Vitagraph*	(1)(S)
Jan 1914	The Romance of Sunshine Alley	*Broncho*	(1)(S)
Dec 1914	Love Will Out	*Vitagraph*	(2)(S)
Jan 1915	The Paris Hat	*Alhambra*	(1)(S)

583 OFFENBACH, Jacques

Oct 1911	The Tales of Hoffmann	*Ouki*	(1)(0)

584 OHNET, Georges

1911	La Fin d'un Jouer	*Film d'Art*	(1)(P)
1912	Countess Sarah	*Film d'Art*	(1)(P)
Dec 1912	The Ironmaster *(Le Maître des Forges)*	*Film d'Art*	(2)(P)
1913	La Grande Marnière	*Film d'Art*	(P)
1913	Serge Panine	*Film d'Art*	(P)
Oct 1914	The Ironmaster *(Le Maître des Forges)*	*Biograph*	(2)(P)
1915	Dette de Haine	*Film d'Art*	(P)
Jul 1915	Dr Rameau	*Fox*	(6)(P)
Sep 1915	The Soul of Pierre	*Biograph*	(3)(P)
Oct 1915	Serge Panine	*Biograph*	(3)(P)
Dec 1915	The Woman of Mystery	*Biograph*	(3)(P)

585 'OLD SCOUT' (pseud.)

Jun 1912	Young Wild West Leading a Raid	*Nestor*	(1)(S)
Jun 1912	Young Wild West on the Border	*Nestor*	(1)(S)
Jul 1912	Young Wild West Cornered by Apaches	*Nestor*	(1)(S)
Jul 1912	Young Wild West Trapping a Tricky Rustler	*Nestor*	(1)(S)
Jul 1912	Young Wild West's Prairie Pursuit	*Nestor*	(1)(S)
Aug 1912	Young Wild West Working Out Gold	*Nestor*	(1)(S)

586 OLIVE, Frank

Feb 1913	The Blacksmith's Story	*Pilot*	(2)(S)

587 OPPENHEIM, Edward Phillips

Apr 1914	The Floor Above *(The Tragedy of Charlecote Mansions)*	*Reliance*	(4)(N)
Mar 1915	The Master Mummer	*Edison*	(3)(N)
Mar 1915	The Black Box	*Universal*	(serial)(N)
Mar 1915	The Master of Merripit	*Clarendon*	(5)(N)
Dec 1915	Mr Grex of Monte Carlo	*Lasky*	(5)(N)

588 OPPENHEIM, James

May 1912	Billie	*Edison*	(1)(S)
Jul 1912	Nerves and the Man *(Daybreak)*	*Edison*	(1)(S)
Nov 1912	Tim	*Edison*	(1)(S)
Nov 1912	Hope	*Edison*	(1)(S)
Nov 1912	The Third Thanksgiving	*Edison*	(1)(S)
Dec 1912	The Curse of Carelessness	*Edison*	(1)(S)
Dec 1912	Annie Crawls Upstairs	*Edison*	(1)(S)
Jan 1913	A Perilous Cargo	*Edison*	(1)(S)
Jan 1913	The Power of Sleep	*Edison*	(1)(S)
Jan 1913	The Man He Might Have Been	*Edison*	(1)(S)
Jan 1913	The Dancer	*Edison*	(1)(S)
Feb 1913	The Phantom Ship	*Edison*	(1)(S)
Dec 1913	Peg o' the Movies	*Edison*	(2)(S)
Oct 1914	Mother o'Dreams	*Essanay*	(2)(S)
Apr 1915	The Stoning	*Edison*	(3)(S)

589 OPPER, Frederick Burr

Nov 1900	Happy Hooligan Assists the Magician	*Edison*	(X)(C)
Apr 1901	Happy Hooligan April Fooled	*Edison*	(X)(C)
Apr 1901	Happy Hooligan Surprised	*Edison*	(X)(C)
Jan 1902	The Twentieth Century Tramp *(Happy Hooligan)*	*Edison*	(X)(C)
Jan 1902	Happy Hooligan Turns Burglar	*Edison*	(X)(C)
Nov 1902	Alphonse and Gaston	*Biograph*	(X)(C)
Nov 1902	Alphonse and Gaston Helping an Irishman	*Biograph*	(X)(C)
Jun 1903	Happy Hooligan	*Biograph*	(X)(C)
Jul 1903	Happy Hooligan in a Trap	*Biograph*	(X)(C)
Jul 1903	Gloomy Gus Gets the Best of It *(Happy Hooligan)*	*Biograph*	(X)(C)
Jul 1903	Happy Hooligan Interferes	*Biograph*	(X)(C)
Jul 1903	An Unprotected Female *(Happy Hooligan)*	*Biograph*	(X)(C)
Aug 1903	Happy Hooligan Earns His Dinner	*Biograph*	(X)(C)
Oct 1903	Happy Hooligan Breaks into Society	*Biograph*	(X)(C)

Oct 1903	Happy Hooligan as a Safe Robber	*Biograph*	(X)(C)
Oct 1903	Happy Hooligan's Interrupted Lunch	*Biograph*	(X)(C)
Oct 1903	Hooligan in Jail	*Biograph*	(X)(C)
Oct 1903	Hooligan to the Rescue	*Biograph*	(X)(C)
Oct 1903	Hooligan's Roller Skates	*Biograph*	(X)(C)
Oct 1903	Alphonse and Gaston No. 3	*Biograph*	(X)(C)
Oct 1903	Alphonse and Gaston Take a Dancing Lesson	*Biograph*	(X)(C)
Oct 1903	Alphonse and Gaston: Next	*Biograph*	(X)(C)
Nov 1903	Poor Hooligan So Hungry Too *(Happy Hooligan)*	*Biograph*	(X)(C)
Nov 1903	Hooligan's Thanksgiving Dinner	*Biograph*	(X)(C)
Dec 1903	Hooligan's Christmas Dream	*Biograph*	(X)(C)
Jun 1914	Happy Hooligan	*Nonpareil*	(1)(C)

590 ORD, Robert

Feb 1916	The King's Outcast *(see also* Mackay, W. Gayer*)*	*London*	(4)(P)

591 OSBORNE, Duffield

Feb 1915	Third Hand High	*Essanay*	(2)(S)

592 OSBORNE, William Hamilton

Jun 1913	The Seal of Silence	*Kaybee*	(2)(S)
Jun 1913	The Boomerang	*Kaybee*	(3)(S)
Jul 1913	The Scapegoat	*American*	(2)(S)
Jul 1913	Henrietta's Hair	*Selig*	(1)(S)
Nov 1913	A Pitfall of the Instalment Plan	*American*	(2)(S)
Jan 1915	Alarm of Angelone	*American*	(2)(S)
Jul 1915	The Running Fight	*Paramount*	(5)(N)
Sep 1915	Infatuation *(see also* Osbourne*)*	*American*	(2)(S)

593 OSBOURNE, Lloyd

Sep 1915	Infatuation *(see also* Osborne, William Hamilton*)*	*American*	(2)(S)

594 OSGOOD, Katherine P.

Dec 1911	Driving Home the Cows	*Kalem*	(1)(S)

595 OUIDA (Louise de la Ramée)

Jul 1912	Under Two Flags	*Gem*	(2)(N)
Jul 1912	Under Two Flags	*Thanhouser*	(2)(N)
Sep 1913	Moths	*Thanhouser*	(5)(N)
Mar 1914	A Dog of Flanders	*Thanhouser*	(2)(N)
May 1915	Strathmore	*Reliance*	(5)(N)
Jul 1915	Under Two Flags	*Biograph*	(3)(N)
Aug 1915	The Little Dutch Girl *(Two Little Wooden Shoes)*	*Shubert*	(5)(N)

596 OUTCAULT, Richard Felton

Oct 1903	Buster's Joke on Papa *(Buster Brown)*	*Edison*	(X)(C)
Mar 1904	Buster Brown	*Edison*	(X)(C)
Dec 1904	Buster and His Dog: Be a Good Boy	*Edison*	(X)(C)
Dec 1904	Buster and His Dog: Buster Quiet	*Edison*	(X)(C)
Dec 1904	Buster and His Dog: Good Dog	*Edison*	(X)(C)
Dec 1904	Buster and His Dog: The Instructions	*Edison*	(X)(C)
Aug 1914	Buster Brown and His Goat	*Edison*	(1)(X)
Sep 1914	Buster Brown on the Care and Treatment of Goats	*Edison*	(1)(X)
Sep 1914	Buster Brown Gets the Worst of It	*Edison*	(1)(C)
Sep 1914	Buster Brown's Education	*Edison*	(1)(C)
Oct 1914	Buster Brown's Uncle	*Edison*	(1)(C)
Oct 1914	Buster Brown Picks Out the Costumes	*Edison*	(1)(C)
Oct 1914	Buster Brown and the German Band	*Edison*	(1)(C)
Nov 1914	Buster Brown Causes a Commotion	*Edison*	(1)(C)

597 OXENHAM, John (William Arthur Dunkerley)

Mar 1915	Hearts in Exile *(see also* Davis, Owen*)*	*Shubert*	(5)(N)

598 OXFORD, John Barton

Oct 1914	Virtue Is Its Own Reward	*Rex*	(2)(S)
Jul 1915	An Hour of Freedom	*Lubin*	(5)(N)

599 OYEN, Henry

Feb 1915	The Dance at Alec Fontaine's	*Essanay*	(1)(S)
Apr 1915	The Snow Burner	*Essanay*	(3)(N)
Aug 1915	The Man Trail	*Essanay*	(6)(N)
Oct 1915	The Outer Edge	*Essanay*	(3)(N)

600 PACKARD, Frank Lucius

Jul 1915	Greater Love Hath No Man	*Popular*	(5)(N)

601 PAGE, Thomas Nelson

Dec 1913	Within the Enemy's Lines *(A Captured Santa Claus)*	*Edison*	(1)(S)
Apr 1915	The Outcast	*Reliance*	(5)(N)

602 PAINE, H. S.

Nov 1912	When Memory Calls *(The Misanthrope Heart)*	*Selig*	(1)(S)

PALMER, Henrietta Eliza Vaughan *see* Winter

603 PARKER, Sir Gilbert

Mar 1912	The House with the Tall Porch	*Edison*	(1)(S)
Mar 1913	The Priest and the Man *(The Going of the White Swan)*	*Edison*	(1)(S)
Mar 1913	The Superior Law *(The Right of Way)*	*Éclair*	(3)(N)
Apr 1913	The Translation of a Savage	*Edison*	(1)(S)
Aug 1913	The Rightful Heir *(The Lane That Had No Turning)*	*Edison*	(1)(S)

May 1914	Pierre of the Plains *(see also* Selwyn*)*	*All Star*	(5)(N)
Sep 1914	The Going of the White Swan	*Selig*	(2)(S)
Oct 1914	The Seats of the Mighty	*Colonial*	(4)(N)
Jul 1915	The Right of Way	*Rolfe*	(5)(N)
Dec 1915	Jordan Is a Hard Road	*Fine Arts*	(5)(N)

604 PARKER, Lottie Blair

Mar 1912	Way Down East	*Solax*	(1)(P)
Aug 1915	Under Southern Skies	*Universal*	(5)(N)

605 PARKER, Louis Napoleon

Dec 1915	Joseph and His Brethren	*Dormet*	(5)(N)

606 PARRISH, Randall

Oct 1915	Yellow Star	*Bison*	(5)(N)

607 PATTERSON, Joseph Medill

Aug 1915	A Little Brother of the Rich	*Bosworth*	(5)(N)

608 PATTULO, George

Feb 1914	Buffalo Jim	*Vitagraph*	(2)(S)
Mar 1914	The Mysterious Shot *(The Higher Law)*	*Reliance*	(2)(S)
Jun 1914	The Rebellion of Kitty Belle	*Majestic*	(2)(S)
Aug 1914	Frenchy	*Majestic*	(2)(S)
Jan 1915	The Better Man	*Majestic*	(2)(S)

609 PAULDING, Frederick

Sep 1913	Trooper Billy	*Kalem*	(2)(S)

610 PAULTON, Harry and Edward

Apr 1915	Niobe	*Famous Players*	(5)(P)

611 PAYNE, John Howard

May 1914	Home, Sweet Home	*Reliance*	(6)(Sg)

612 PEARSON, Hesketh

Nov 1912	Don Q: The Dark Brothers of the Civil Guard	*B & C*	(1)(S)
Nov 1912	Don Q: How He Outwitted Don Louis	*B & C*	(1)(S)
Dec 1912	Don Q and the Artist	*B & C*	(1)(S)
Dec 1912	Don Q: How He Treated the Pardon of Gevil Hay	*B & C*	(1)(S)
Apr 1914	The Cage	*London*	(2)(S)

613 PECK, George Wilbur

May 1908	Peck's Bad Boy	*Essanay*	(1)(S)

614 PEMBERTON, Sir Max

Nov 1913	David Garrick (*see also* Robertson)	*Zenith*	(2)(P)
Jun 1914	Kronstadt	*Gaumont*	(3)(P)
Nov 1915	In Search of a Husband	*Clarendon*	(3)(P)

615 PENDER, Bob

Nov 1904	Hands Up	*Gaumont*	(X)(P)

616 PEPLE, Edward Henry

Apr 1914	The Littlest Rebel	*Photoplay*	(5)(N)
Jun 1914	The Spitfire	*Famous Players*	(4)(N)
Mar 1915	The Love Route Via Pitman	*Essanay*	(4)(S)

617 PERRAULT, Charles

Aug 1898	Cinderella and the Fairy Godmother	*Smith*	(X)(S)
Oct 1899	Cinderella	*Méliès*	(X)(S)
May 1903	Puss in Boots	*Lubin*	(X)(S)
Nov 1904	Puss in Boots	*Pathé*	(X)(S)
1905	Cinderella	*Méliès*	(1)(S)
Feb 1907	Cinderella	*Pathé*	(1)(S)
Dec 1907	Cinderella	*Hepworth*	(1)(S)
Mar 1908	The Sleeping Beauty	*Pathé*	(1)(S)
Dec 1908	Tom Thumb	*Pathé*	(1)(S)
Nov 1909	Blue Beard	*Edison*	(X)(S)
Dec 1911	Cinderella	*Selig*	(1)(S)
Dec 1911	Cinderella	*Thanhouser*	(1)(S)
Dec 1911	Cinderella	*Méliès*	(1)(S)
Aug 1912	Hop O' My Thumb	*Gaumont*	(1)(S)
Dec 1912	Sleeping Beauty	*Close*	(1)(S)
Feb 1913	Cinderella's Slipper (*Cinderella)*	*Vitagraph*	(1)(S)
Dec 1913	Cinderella	*Ambrosio*	(2)(S)
Dec 1913	Cinderella (*see also* Rideout)	*Hepworth*	(1)(S)
Jan 1915	Cinderella	*Famous Players*	(5)(S)

618 PETTIT, Henry (*see also* Sims)

Sep 1914	Harbour Lights	*Neptune*	(3)(P)
Dec 1914	In the Ranks	*Neptune*	(4)(P)
May 1915	Master and Man	*Neptune*	(4)(P)

619 PEZET, Alfonso Washington

Aug 1915	Marrying Money (*see also* Marburgh)	*Shubert*	(5)(P)

620 PHELPS, Elizabeth Stuart

Dec 1911 Pull for the Shore, Sailor *Edison* (1)(S)
(The Madonna of the Tubs)

621 PHILIPPE, D.

Jun 1903 Remorse *Williamson* (X)(P)

622 PHILIPPS, F.C.

Mar 1913 As in a Looking Glass *Monopol* (2)(S)

623 PHILLIPS, David Graham

Jan 1915 A Grain of Dust *Fox* (5)(N)

624 PHILLIPS, Watts

Aug 1914 The Dead Heart *Hepworth* (3)(P)

625 PIATTI, P.G.

Sep 1914 The Lion of Venice *Ambrosio* (N)
(La Foscari)

626 PIDGIN, Charles Felton

Dec 1912 Quincy Adams Sawyer *Puritan* (1)(S)
(see also Adams, Frederic Justin*)*

627 PINERO, Sir Arthur Wing

Nov 1914 The Second Mrs Tanqueray *Biograph* (2)(P)
Oct 1915 Sweet Lavender *Hepworth* (5)(P)
Nov 1915 Iris *Hepworth* (5)(P)

628 PLEON, Harry

Jan 1914 The Importance of Being Another Man's Wife *Hepworth* (2)(P)

629 POE, Edgar Allan

1907	The Bells	*Vitagraph*	(1)(Pm)
Feb 1909	Edgar Allen Poe *(The Raven)*	*Biograph*	(1)(Pm)
May 1909	Lunatics in Power *(The System of Dr Tarr and Professor Fether)*	*Edison*	(1)(S)
Sep 1909	The Sealed Room *(The Cask of Amontillado)*	*Biograph*	(X)(S)
Feb 1910	The Pit and the Pendulum	*Ambrosio*	(X)(S)
Feb 1910	Hop-Frog the Jester *(Hop-Frog)*	*Ambrosio*	(X)(S)
May 1912	The Raven	*Éclair*	(1)(Pm)
Jul 1913	The Pit and the Pendulum	*Solax*	(2)(S)
Jul 1913	The Bells	*Edison*	(1)(Pm)
Aug 1914	The Murders in the Rue Morgue	*Rosenberg*	(2)(S)
Aug 1914	The Avenging Conscience *(The Tell-Tale Heart)*	*Griffith*	(8)(S)
Aug 1915	The Tides of Time *(The Conqueror Worm)*	*Knickerbocker*	(3)(Pm)
Oct 1915	The Raven (*see also* Hazelton)	*Essanay*	(6)(Pm)

630 POLLOCK, Channing

Sep 1913	In The Bishop's Carriage (*see also* Michelson)	*Famous Players*	(5)(P)
Mar 1914	Clothes (*see also* Hopwood)	*Famous Players*	(4)(P)
Jul 1914	The Little Gray Lady	*Famous Players*	(4)(P)
Sep 1914	Such a Little Queen	*Famous Players*	(4)(P)
Oct 1914	The Pit	*Brady*	(5)(N)
Jun 1915	My Best Girl (*see also* Wolf)	*Rolfe*	(5)(N)
Aug 1915	The Secret Orchard (*see also* Castle)	*Lasky*	(5)(N)

POQUELIN, Jean-Baptiste *see* Molière

631 PORTER, Gene Stratton (Geneva Grace Stratton Porter)

Oct 1909	Laddie	*Edison*	(4)(N)

Porter, William Sydney *see* Henry

632 POTTER, Paul M.

May 1914	The Conquerors	*Ramo*	(5)(N)

633 POYNTER, Beulah

Jan 1915	The Little Girl That He Forgot	*Cosmos*	(5)(N)

634 PRATT, William W. (*see also* Arthur, Timothy Shay)

May 1903	Ten Nights in a Barroom	*Biograph*	(X)(N)
Oct 1903	Ten Nights in a Barroom	*Lubin*	(X)(N)
Jun 1909	Ten Nights in a Barroom	*Essanay*	(1)(N)
Oct 1910	Ten Nights in a Barroom	*Thanhouser*	(1)(N)
Jun 1911	Ten Nights in a Barroom	*Selig*	(1)(N)
Nov 1913	Ten Nights in a Barroom	*Photo Drama*	(4)(N)
Jul 1915	Not Much Force	*Edison*	(1)(S)

635 PRESCOTT, William Hickling

May 1910	The Aztec Sacrifice *(The Conquest of Mexico)*	*Kalem*	(1)(NF)

636 PRÉVOST, Antoine–François

Jan 1910	Manon	*Pathé*	(1)(N)
1911	Manon Lescaut	*SCAGL*	(1)(N)
Feb 1914	Manon Lescaut (*see also* Massenet)	*Playgoers*	(6)(N)

PRICE, Ellen *see* Wood, Mrs Henry

637 PROCTOR, Adelaide Anne

Oct 1913	The Trail of the Lost Chord *(A Lost Chord)*	*American*	(1)(S)
Nov 1913	The Legend of Provence	*Thanhouser*	(1)(S)

638 PUCCINI, Giacomo

1913	La Vie de Bohème *(see also* Murger*)*	*SCAGL*	(2)(0)

PUDDICOMBE, Anne *see* Raine, Allen

639 QUICK, Herbert

Nov 1915	Double Trouble	*Fine Arts*	(5)(N)

640 RACEWARD, Thomas

Jul 1915	Sunday	*Filmotions*	(4)(S)

641 RACINE, Jean

1908	Athalie	*SCAGL*	(X)(P)
1910	Athalie	*Film d'Art*	(1)(P)
1910	Phaedra *(Phèdre)*	*Itala*	(1)(P)

642 RAINE, Allen (Anne Adaliza Puddicombe)

Dec 1915	A Welsh Singer	*Turner*	(5)(N)

643 RAINE, William McLeod

Nov 1913	The Face of Fear	*Vitagraph*	(1)(S)
Jan 1915	Forked Trails	*Selig*	(1)(S)
Feb 1915	Ridgeway of Montana	*Bison*	(3)(S)
Apr 1915	An Arizona Wooing	*Selig*	(1)(S)
Jun 1915	An Intercepted Vengeance	*Vitagraph*	(1)(S)
Jun 1915	All on Account of Towser	*Vitagraph*	(1)(S)
Aug 1915	Through Troubled Waters	*Vitagraph*	(3)(N)

644 RALEIGH, Cecil

Oct 1914	The King's Minister	*London*	(3)(P)
Jan 1915	The Sporting Duchess	*Lubin*	(4)(P)
May 1915	The Great Ruby *(see also* Hamilton, Henry*)*	*Lubin*	(5)(P)
Jul 1915	The Derby Winner *(see also* Hamilton, Henry*)*	*London*	(5)(P)
Dec 1915	The Sins of Society *(see also* Hamilton, Henry*)*	*Brady*	(5)(P)

645 RANKIN, McKee

Jan 1912	The Dainties	*Selig*	(2)(S)
Jul 1915	The Runaway Wife	*Kalem*	(5)(N)

646 RASMUS, Miriam Bode

Oct 1914	Her Life's Story	*Rex*	(2)(S)

647 RAYNER, Barnabas

Dec 1908	The Dumb Man of Manchester	*Haggar*	(1)(P)

648 READ, Opie Percival

Nov 1912	The Starbucks *(The Tennessee Judge)*	*American*	(2)(N)
Sep 1915	A Yankee from the West	*Majestic*	(5)(N)

649 READE, Charles

Jul 1910	Peg Woffington	*Edison*	(1)(N)
Apr 1911	Turned to the Wall *(Put Yourself in His Place)*	*Edison*	(1)(N)
Sep 1911	Foul Play	*Edison*	(1)(P)
Jun 1912	It's Never Too Late To Mend *(It is Never Too Late To Mend)*	*Imp*	(2)(N)
Aug 1912	Peg Woffington *(see also* Taylor, Tom*)*	*Britannia*	(2)(N)

Oct 1912	Put Yourself in His Place	*Thanhouser*	(2)(N)
Jan 1913	It's Never Too Late To Mend *(It is Never Too Late To Mend)*	*Edison*	(2)(N)
Sep 1913	Hard Cash	*Edison*	(2)(N)
Nov 1913	The Cloister and the Hearth	*Hepworth*	(5)(N)
Jul 1914	Detective Craig's Coup *(The Ticket-of-Leave Man)*	*Eclectic*	(5)(P)
Oct 1914	The Ticket-of-Leave Man	*Wharton*	(3)(P)
Oct 1914	Masks and Faces *(Peg Woffington)*	*Biograph*	(2)(P)
Apr 1915	The True Story of the Lyons Mail *(The Courier of Lyons)(see also* Moreau, Eugène*)*	*Samuelson*	(2)(P)

650 REED, Haines W.

Mar 1915	The Mother Instinct	*Bison*	(3)(S)

651 REEVE, Arthur Benjamin

Dec 1914	The Exploits of Elaine	*Pathé*	(serial)(N)

652 REID, Hal

Sep 1911	Joe and Jim	*Selig*	(1)(S)
Jan 1912	An Indian Romeo and Juliet	*Vitagraph*	(1)(S)
Jul 1912	At Cripple Creek	*Reliance*	(2)(S)
Sep 1912	Human Hearts	*Imp*	(2)(P)
Oct 1912	Sue	*Champion*	(1)(S)
Jan 1913	Thou Shalt Not Kill	*Vitagraph*	(1)(P)
Jul 1914	Dan	*All Star*	(5)(P)
Nov 1914	Human Hearts	*Imp*	(3)(P)
Dec 1914	Heart of the Hills	*Victor*	(3)(P)
Jan 1915	Time Lock Number 776	*Photo Drama*	(5)(P)
Mar 1915	Prohibition	*Prohibition*	(4)(P)
Jun 1915	The Highwayman	*Vitagraph*	(1)(S)
Dec 1915	Thou Shalt Not Kill	*Circle*	(5)(P)

653 REINHART, John

Jul 1914	The Scales of Justice	*Famous Players*	(5)(P)

654 RENAUD, J. J.

Aug 1913	The Rajah's Diamond Rose	*Eclipse*	(2)(S)

655 REYNOLDS, Stephen Allen

May 1913	The Master Cracksman	*Reliance*	(2)(S)

656 RHOADES, Nina

Sep 1912	The Little Girl Next Door	*Edison*	(1)(S)

657 RHODES, Eugene Manlove

Mar 1914	Sealed Orders	*Universal*	(2)(N)
Jun 1914	The Blunderer's Mask	*Éclair*	(1)(S)
Aug 1914	Bransford in Arcadia *(The Little Eohippus)*	*Éclair*	(4)(N)
Dec 1914	Within an Inch of His Life	*Éclair*	(2)(S)
Feb 1915	The Awaited Hour	*Imp*	(2)(S)
Mar 1915	The Long Shift	*United*	(4)(N)
Sep 1915	The Fool's Heart	*Éclair*	(4)(N)

658 RHODES, Harrison Garfield

Oct 1914	The Gentleman from Mississippi *(see also* Wise*)*	*Brady*	(5)(N)

659 RICE, Alice Hegan

Nov 1914	Mrs Wiggs of the Cabbage Patch *(see also* Flexner*)*	*California*	(5)(N)

660 RICHARDSON, Abby Sage

Feb 1914	The Pride of Jennico *(see also* Furniss*)*	*Famous Players*	(4)(P)

661 RIDEOUT, Herbert C.

Dec 1913	Cinderella *(see also* Perrault*)*	*Hepworth*	(1)(P)

662 RIGBY, Freddie

May 1914	Buying a Horse	*Lucrative*	(X)(P)
May 1914	Billposting	*Lucrative*	(X)(P)

663 RILEY, James Whitcomb

May 1910	There, Little Girl, Don't Cry *(A Life's Story)*	*Selig*	(1)(Pm)
Feb 1911	The Old Man and Jim	*Champion*	(1)(Pm)
Oct 1911	An Old Sweetheart of Mine	*Edison*	(1)(Pm)
Jul 1912	When She Was About Sixteen	*Edison*	(1)(Pm)

664 RILEY, Madeleine Lucette

Jan 1914	An American Citizen	*Famous Players*	(4)(P)
Jun 1915	Mice And Men	*Famous Players*	(5)(P)

665 RINEHART, Mary Roberts

Jun 1914	Jane	*Essanay*	(1)(S)
Aug 1915	The Cave on Thundercloud	*Essanay*	(1)(S)
Sep 1915	Mind Over Motor	*Essanay*	(1)(S)
Sep 1915	Tish's Spy	*Essanay*	(3)(S)
Sep 1915	The Circular Staircase	*Selig*	(5)(N)
Sep 1915	Affinities	*Essanay*	(2)(S)
Nov 1915	The Papered Door	*Essanay*	(3)(S)
Dec 1915	What Happened to Father	*Vitagraph*	(5)(N)

666 RISQUE, W. H.

Jun 1901	Tally-Ho	*Gibbons*	(X)(P)

667 RITA (Eliza Margaret Humphreys)

Jan 1914	The Haunted Bedroom	*Edison*	(1)(S)
Aug 1914	The Mysterious Lodger	*Vitagraph*	(1)(S)
Aug 1915	A Park Lane Scandal	*MLB*	(2)(N)

668 RIVES, Hallie Erminia

Mar 1915	Satan Sanderson	*Rolfe*	(5)(N)

669 ROBERTS, Alice M.

Nov 1914	When Fate Leads Trump (*see also* Hymer)	*Excelsior*	(4)(S)
Apr 1915	The Grim Messenger	*Universal*	(2)(S)

670 ROBERTS, George

Apr 1915	A Deadly Hate	*Edison*	(3)(S)

671 ROBERTSON, Thomas William

Oct 1908	David Garrick	*Essanay*	(1)(P)
Oct 1912	David Garrick	*London*	(1)(P)
Dec 1912	David Garrick	*Ruffells*	(2)(P)
Mar 1913	The Fugitive (*The Young Collegian*)	*Selig*	(2)(P)
Sep 1913	Caste	*Edison*	(2)(P)
Sep 1913	David Garrick (*see also* Pemberton)	*Zenith*	(2)(P)
Dec 1913	David Garrick	*Hepworth*	(4)(P)
Jul 1914	David Garrick	*Vitagraph*	(4)(P)
Oct 1915	Caste	*Turner*	(5)(P)

672 ROE, Virgie E.

Jul 1915	Her Idol *(A Phoenix of the Hills)*	*Lubin*	(5)(N)

673 ROMA, Roma T.

Aug 1898	He and She	*Biograph*	(X)(P)

674 ROSE, Edward Everett

Sep 1900	English Nell *(see also* Hope*)*	*Biograph*	(X)(P)
Jul 1913	Her Rosary *(The Rosary)*	*Reliance*	(2)(P)
Mar 1914	The Prisoner of Zenda *(see also* Hope*)*	*London*	(5)(P)
Jun 1915	The Rosary *(see also* Barclay*)*	*Selig*	(7)(P)
Oct 1915	Under the Red Robe *(see also* Weyman*)*	*Clarendon*	(4)(P)
Jun 1915	Fighting Bob	*Rolfe*	(5)(P)

675 ROSI, G. V.

Dec 1904	A Pierrot's Romance	*Urban*	(X)(P)

676 ROSS, Charles Henry

Jul 1898	Sloper's Visit to Brighton	*Williamson*	(X)(C)
Oct 1898	Ally Sloper	*Smith*	(X)(C)

677 ROSSINI, Gioacchino Antonio

1904	The Barber of Seville	*Méliès*	(X)(O)
1910	The Barber of Seville	*Pathé*	(X)(O)
1910	The Barber of Seville	*Ambrosio*	(1)(O)

678 ROSTAND, Edmond

Jan 1909	Cyrano de Bergerac	*Lux*	(1)(P)
Sep 1911	Adventures of Cyrano de Bergerac *(Cyrano de Bergerac)*	*Pathé*	(2)(P)
Jul 1914	L'Aiglon	*Éclair*	(10)(P)

679 ROSTAND, Maurice

Feb 1914	A Good Little Devil *(see also* Gerard; Strong*)*	*Famous Players*	(5)(P)

680 ROWE, Nicholas

Aug 1908	Jane Shore	*Gaumont*	(X)(P)
Oct 1911	Jane Shore	*Britannia*	(1)(P)
May 1915	Jane Shore *(see also* Wills*)*	*Barker*	(6)(P)

681 ROWLAND, Henry Cottrell

Jun 1915	Braga's Double	*Essanay*	(2)(S)
Jul 1915	The Rajah's Tunic	*Essanay*	(2)(S)
Jul 1915	Jabez's Conquest	*Essanay*	(2)(S)
Aug 1915	Business Rivals	*Essanay*	(2)(S)
Aug 1915	The Adventures of Domenica	*Essanay*	(2)(S)
Aug 1915	Legrand's Revenge	*Essanay*	(2)(S)
Aug 1915	The Return of Gentleman Joe	*Essanay*	(2)(S)
Oct 1915	The Closing Net	*Pathé*	(5)(S)

682 ROYLE, Edward Milton

Feb 1914	The Squaw Man *(see also* Belasco*)*	*Lasky*	(6)(P)
Nov 1915	The Unwritten Law	*California*	(5)(P)

683 RUSSELL, Sol Smith

Dec 1915	A Poor Relation	*Biograph*	(30(S)

684 RYER, George W.

Nov 1913	Our New Minister	*Kalem*	(3)(S)

685 SAND, George (Amandine Aurore Dupin, Baronne Dudevant)

Jun 1912	Fanchon the Cricket	*Imp*	(2)(N)
May 1915	Fanchon the Cricket	*Famous Players*	(5)(N)
Jun 1915	The Twelfth Hour *(Fanchon the Cricket)*	*Imp*	(5)(N)

686 SARDOU, Victorien

1908	Tosca	*Nordisk*	(1)(P)
1909	Divorçons	*Nordisk*	(1)(P)
Dec 1909	Madame Sans-Gêne	*Nordisk*	(1)(P)
1909	La Tosca	*Pathé*	(1)(P)
1911	La Tosca	*Film d'Art*	(1)(P)
1911	Madame Tallien	*SCAGL*	(1)(P)
Dec 1911	Madame Sans-Gêne	*Film d'Art*	(1)(P)
1912	Adrienne Lecouvreur *(see also* Legouvé; Scribe*)*	*SCAGL*	(2)(P)
Jan 1912	Divorçons	*Éclair*	(2)(P)
1912	Theodora	*Film d'Art*	(2)(P)
Sep 1912	La Tosca	*Éclair*	(2)(P)
Jan 1913	Cleopatra	*Gardner*	(6)(P)
Feb 1913	Theodora	*Aquila*	(3)(P)
Jul 1914	Pro Patria	*SCAGL*	(5)(P)
May 1915	Princess Romanoff *(Theodora)(see also* Traut*)*	*Fox*	(6)(P)
Dec 1915	Divorçons	*Biograph*	(4)(P)

687 SARTENE, Jean

Oct 1913	The Grip *(La Griffe)*	*Britannic*	(4)(P)

688 SAVAGE, Richard Henry

Jun 1914	My Official Wife *(see also* Gunter*)*	*Vitagraph*	(5)(N)

689 SAYRE, Theodore Burt

Mar 1915	The Commanding Officer	*Famous Players*	(5)(P)

690 SAZIE, Leon

1911	Zigomar, King of Thieves	*Éclair*	(1)(S)
1911	Zigomar Versus Nick Carter *(see also* Carter, Nick*)*	*Éclair*	(1)(S)
1911	Zigomar, The Eel's Skin	*Éclair*	(1)(S)

691 SCARBOROUGH, George

Jul 1914	The Lure	*Shubert*	(6)(N)
Oct 1915	The Final Judgment	*Rolfe*	(5)(N)
Nov 1915	At Bay	*Pathé*	(5)(N)

692 SCHILLER, Johann Christoph Friedrich von

Sep 1909	The Bell	*Cines*	(X)(S)
Oct 1909	The Hostage	*Ambrosio*	(X)(S)
Jul 1910	Louisa Muller	*Itala*	(1)(S)
Oct 1911	Fridolin	*Gaumont*	(1)(S)
May 1913	Mary Stuart	*Edison*	(3)(P)
Aug 1913	The Robbers	*Edison*	(1)(S)
May 1914	William Tell	*Greene*	(6)(P)
Nov 1914	The Robbers	*Cosmopolitan*	(6)(S)
Dec 1914	The Robbers	*Leemund*	(5)(S)

693 SCHULTZE, Charles

May 1902	The Creators of Foxy Grandpa	*Biograph*	(X)(C)
May 1902	The Boys Try to Put One up on Foxy Grandpa	*Biograph*	(X)(C)

May 1902	Foxy Grandpa and Polly in a Little Hilarity	*Biograph*	(X)(C)
May 1902	Foxy Grandpa Shows the Boys a Trick or Two	*Biograph*	(X)(C)
May 1902	Foxy Grandpa Tells the Boys a Funny Story	*Biograph*	(X)(C)
May 1902	The Boys Help Themselves to Foxy Grandpa's Cigars	*Biograph*	(X)(C)
May 1902	The Boys Still Determined Try It Again on Foxy Grandpa	*Biograph*	(X)(C)
May 1902	The Boys Think They Have One on Foxy Grandpa But He Fools Them	*Biograph*	(X)(C)
Jul 1903	Why Foxy Grandpa Escaped a Ducking	*Biograph*	(X)(C)

694 SCOTT, Clement William

Sep 1914	Poppies *(In Poppyland)(see also* De Lana*)*	*Climax*	(1)(Pm)

695 SCOTT, John Reed

Dec 1914	The Colonel of the Red Hussars	*Edison*	(3)(S)

696 SCOTT, Leroy

Nov 1914	The Odalisque	*Majestic*	(2)(S)

697 SCOTT, Malcolm

Nov 1913	How a Housekeeper Lost Her Character	*Magnet*	(1)(P)

698 SCOTT, Michael

Apr 1913	Tom Cringle in Jamaica *(Tom Cringle's Log)*	*B & C*	(1)(N)

699 SCOTT, Sir Walter

Dec 1908	Lucia Di Lammermoor *(The Bride of Lammermoor)(see also* Donizetti*)*	*Itala*	(X)(N)
1908	Lucia Di Lammermoor *(The Bride of Lammermoor)(see also* Donizetti*)*	*Ambrosio*	(X)(N)
Dec 1908	The Bride of Lammermoor	*Vitagraph*	(X)(N)
Feb 1909	Kenilworth	*Vitagraph*	(X)(N)
Jul 1909	Lochinvar	*Edison*	(X)(Pm)
Apr 1910	The Death of Charles the Bold *(Anne of Geierstein)*	*Pathé*	(X)(N)
Oct 1910	The Bride of Lammermoor	*Cines*	(1)(N)
1911	An Adventure of Rob Roy *(Rob Roy)*	*Gaumont*	(1)(N)
Sep 1911	Rob Roy	*United*	(3)(N)
Sep 1911	Lochinvar	*Thanhouser*	(1)(Pm)
Dec 1911	Quentin Durward	*SCAGL*	(1)(N)
May 1912	The Lady of the Lake	*Vitagraph*	(1)(Pm)
Aug 1912	Richard the Lion-hearted *(The Talisman)*	*Cines*	(2)(N)
Aug 1912	The Bride of Lammermoor	*Cines*	(1)(N)
Oct 1912	Guy Mannering	*Reliance*	(2)(N)
Sep 1913	Rob Roy	*Éclair*	(2)(N)
Sep 1913	Ivanhoe	*Imp*	(3)(N)
Sep 1913	Ivanhoe *(see also* Melville*)*	*Zenith*	(6)(N)
Nov 1913	The Lady of the Lake	*Juno*	(3)(Pm)
Jan 1914	The Bride of Lammermoor	*Kennedy*	(3)(N)
Apr 1914	The Heart of Midlothian	*Hepworth*	(4)(N)
May 1914	A Woman's Triumph *(The Heart of Midlothian)*	*Famous Players*	(4)(N)
Aug 1915	Lochinvar	*Gaumont*	(2)(Pm)

700 SCRIBE, Augustin Eugène

May 1910	Fra Diavolo *(see also* Auber*)*	*Pathé*	(1)(P)
1912	Adrienne Lecouvreur *(see also* Legouvé; Sardou*)*	*Film d'Art*	(2)(P)

701 SELBY, Charles

Aug 1913	London by Night	*Barker*	(3)(P)

702 SELWYN, Edgar

Feb 1914	The Country Boy	*Lasky*	(5)(N)
Apr 1914	Pierre of the Plains *(see also* Parker, Sir Gilbert*)*	*All Star*	(5)(N)
Jun 1915	The Arab	*Lasky*	(5)(N)

703 SERVICE, Robert William

May 1915	The Shooting of Dan McGrew	*Popular*	(5)(Pm)
Oct 1915	The Song of the Wage Slave	*Popular*	(5)(Pm)
Oct 1915	My Madonna	*Popular*	(5)(Pm)

704 SHAKESPEARE, William

Sep 1899	King John	*Biograph*	(X)(P)
Jul 1905	Duel Scene from Macbeth *(Macbeth)*	*Biograph*	(X)(P)
Oct 1905	The Tempest	*Urban*	(X)(P)
Oct 1906	Othello	*Pathé*	(X)(P)
Oct 1907	Hamlet	*Méliès*	(1)(P)
Nov 1907	The Death of Julius Caesar *(Julius Caesar)*	*Méliès*	(X)(P)
Mar 1908	Julius Caesar	*Lubin*	(1)(P)
Apr 1908	Macbeth	*Vitagraph*	(1)(P)
Apr 1908	Romeo and Juliet	*Cines*	(1)(P)
May 1908	Romeo and Juliet	*Vitagraph*	(1)(P)
Jun 1908	Romeo and Juliet	*Gaumont*	(1)(P)
Jul 1908	Othello	*Nordisk*	(X)(P)
Aug 1908	As You Like It	*Kalem*	(1)(P)
Sep 1908	Richard III	*Vitagraph*	(1)(P)
Oct 1908	Antony and Cleopatra	*Vitagraph*	(1)(P)
Nov 1908	The Taming of the Shrew	*Biograph*	(1)(P)
Nov 1908	The Tempest	*Clarendon*	(X)(P)
1908	Hamlet	*SCAGL*	(1)(P)

1908	Hamlet	*Cines*	(1)(P)
1908	Macbeth	*SCAGL*	(1)(P)
Dec 1908	Julius Caesar	*Vitagraph*	(1)(P)
Aug 1909	Brutus *(Julius Caesar)*	*Itala*	(1)(P)
Aug 1909	Othello, The Moor of Venice *(Othello)*	*Pathé*	(1)(P)
Sep 1909	Macbeth	*Cines*	(1)(P)
Oct 1909	A Midsummer Night's Dream	*Lion*	(1)(P)
Nov 1909	Hamlet	*Lux*	(1)(P)
Nov 1909	A Winter's Tale *(The Winter's Tale)*	*Edison*	(1)(P)
Dec 1909	A Midsummer Night's Dream	*Vitagraph*	(1)(P)
Feb 1910	Twelfth Night	*Vitagraph*	(1)(P)
Feb 1910	A Winter's Tale *(The Winter's Tale)*	*Cines*	(1)(P)
Apr 1910	King Lear	*Pasquali*	(1)(P)
May 1910	Winter's Tale *(The Winter's Tale)*	*Thanhouser*	(1)(P)
Oct 1910	Macbeth	*Film d'Art*	(1)(P)
1910	Romeo and Juliet	*Selig*	(1)(P)
1910	Hamlet	*Film d'Art*	(1)(P)
Oct 1910	King Lear	*Film d'Art*	(1)(P)
Nov 1910	The Merry Wives of Windsor	*Selig*	(1)(P)
Dec 1910	The Merchant of Venice	*Film d'Art*	(1)(P)
Jan 1911	Hamlet	*Nordisk*	(1)(P)
Feb 1911	Henry VIII	*Barker*	(2)(P)
Mar 1911	Falstaff *(The Merry Wives of Windsor)*	*Eclipse*	(1)(P)
Mar 1911	Julius Caesar	*Cooperative*	(1)(P)
Apr 1911	Macbeth	*Cooperative*	(1)(P)
Apr 1911	The Taming of the Shrew	*Cooperative*	(1)(P)
May 1911	The Taming of the Shrew	*Eclipse*	(1)(P)
May 1911	Richard III	*Cooperative*	(1)(P)
Aug 1911	Romeo and Juliet	*Thanhouser*	(1)(P)
Nov 1911	The Tempest	*Thanhouser*	(1)(P)
Jan 1912	Brutus *(Julius Caesar)*	*Cines*	(1)(P)

Mar 1912	Hamlet	*Barker*	(2)(P)
Jul 1912	As You Like It	*Vitagraph*	(3)(P)
Jul 1912	The Merchant of Venice	*Thanhouser*	(2)(P)
Nov 1912	The Tempest	*Éclair*	(2)(P)
Dec 1912	Romeo and Juliet	*Pathé*	(3)(P)
Feb 1913	Shylock *(The Merchant of Venice)*	*SCAGL*	(2)(P)
Mar 1913	Cymbeline	*Thanhouser*	(2)(P)
Apr 1913	The Tempest	*Union*	(2)(P)
Apr 1913	Richard III	*Shakespeare*	(P)
Aug 1913	Antony and Cleopatra	*Cines*	(8)(P)
Sep 1913	Macbeth	*F.G.*	(P)
Sep 1913	Richard III	*Starling*	(P)
Oct 1913	Hamlet	*Hepworth*	(6)(P)
1913	A Tragedy of the Sicilian Court *(The Winter's Tale)*	*Milano*	(3)(P)
Feb 1914	The Merchant of Venice	*Rex*	(4)(P)
May 1914	Antony and Cleopatra	*Pathé*	(2)(P)
Jun 1914	The Seven Ages of Man *(As You Like It)*	*Planet*	(1)(Pm)
Jul 1914	Othello	*Cines*	(5)(P)
Aug 1914	Hamlet	*Vitagraph*	(5)(P)
Sep 1914	Hamlet	*Williams*	(1)(P)
Sep 1914	Hubert and Arthur *(King John)*	*Williams*	(1)(P)
Nov 1914	Julius Caesar	*Kleine*	(4)(P)
1914	Othello	*Ambrosio*	(4)(P)
Jun 1915	The Taming of the Shrew	*B & C*	(2)(P)
Jul 1915	England's Warrior King *(Henry V)*	*Williams*	(1)(P)
Nov 1915	Love in a Wood *(As You Like It)*	*Diploma*	(4)(P)

705 SHAW, George Bernard

Nov 1914	The Chocolate Soldier *(Arms and the Man)(see also* Straus*)*	*Whitney*	(5)(P)

706 SHEA, Thomas E.

Sep 1914	The Man O' War's Man	*Broadway*	(5)(P)

707 SHEDD, George Clifford

Sep 1915	The Incorrigible Dukane	*Famous Players*	(5)(P)

708 SHEEHAN, Perley Poore

Dec 1915	The Dragon	*Equitable*	(5)(N)

709 SHELDON, Edward Brewster

May 1915	The High Road	*Rolfe*	(5)(P)
May 1915	The Boss	*World*	(5)(P)
Jul 1915	The Nigger *(The Governor)*	*Fox*	(5)(P)
Aug 1915	Salvation Nell	*California*	(5)(P)

710 SHELDON, H. S.

Jun 1914	Captain Alvarez	*Vitagraph*	(6)(N)
May 1915	Frauds	*Essanay*	(2)(N)
May 1915	Means and Morals	*Essanay*	(2)(N)
Sep 1915	The Circular Path	*Essanay*	(3)(N)
Sep 1915	The House Divided	*Essanay*	(3)(N)
Nov 1915	A Daughter of the City	*Essanay*	(5)(N)

711 SHELLEY, Mary Wollstonecraft

Mar 1910	Frankenstein	*Edison*	(1)(N)
1915	Life Without Soul *(Frankenstein)*	*Ocean*	(5)(N)

712 SHERIDAN, Richard Brinsley

Sep 1913	The Rivals	*Kinemacolor*	(2)(P)
Sep 1914	The Rivals	*Williams*	(1)(P)

Dec 1914	The School for Scandal	*Kalem*	(4)(P)

713 SHIRLEY, Arthur

Nov 1908	Saved from the Sea (*see also* Landeck)	*Gaumont*	(X)(P)
Apr 1910	Tommy Atkins (*see also* Landeck)	*Gaumont*	(1)(P)
Jul 1913	The Grip of Iron	*Brightonia*	(3)(P)
Aug 1914	The King of Crime	*Magnet*	(4)(P)
Jan 1915	Tommy Atkins (*see also* Landeck)	*Barker*	(4)(P)
May 1915	The Bottle (*see also* Cruikshank)	*Hepworth*	(3)(P)
May 1915	The Model	*World*	(5)(P)
Jun 1915	My Old Dutch (*see also* Chevalier)	*Turner*	(5)(P)
Sep 1915	Jack Tar (*see also* Landeck)	*Barker*	(5)(P)
Dec 1915	Her Life in London	*Martin*	(4)(P)

714 SHORE, Dorothy G.

Oct 1912	The Land Beyond the Sunset	*Edison*	(1)(S)

715 SIENKIEWICZ, HENRYK

Dec 1904	Quo Vadis	*Pathé*	(X)(N)
1910	En Temps des Premiers Chrétiens (*Quo Vadis*)	*Film d'Art*	(1)(N)
Dec 1912	Quo Vadis	*Cines*	(1)(N)
Apr 1913	Quo Vadis	*Kleine*	(8)(N)

716 SILBY, Charles

May 1913	The Marble Heart	*Thanhouser*	(2)(S)

717 SIMS, George R.

Jun 1908	Ostler Joe	*Biograph*	(X)(Pm)
Nov 1908	Lady Letmere's Jewellery	*Gaumont*	(1)(S)
Nov 1911	The Price *(Ostler Joe)*	*Rex*	(1)(Pm)
Sep 1912	Ostler Joe	*Edison*	(1)(Pm)
Oct 1912	Ostler Joe	*Comet*	(1)(Pm)
Apr 1914	The Lights O' London	*Barker*	(4)(P)
Apr 1914	The Lifeboat	*Williams*	(1)(Pm)
Jun 1914	The Lights O' London	*World*	(5)(P)
Jul 1914	The Romany Rye	*Leonard*	(4)(P)
Sep 1914	Harbour Lights *(see also* Pettit*)*	*Neptune*	(3)(P)
Nov 1914	Christmas Day in the Workhouse	*Samuelson*	(1)(Pm)
Dec 1914	In the Ranks *(see also* Pettit*)*	*Neptune*	(4)(P)
Mar 1915	The Romany Rye	*Neptune*	(3)(P)
Apr 1915	The Trumpet Call *(see also* Buchanan, Robert*)*	*Neptune*	(4)(P)
May 1915	Master and Man *(see also* Pettit*)*	*Neptune*	(4)(P)
Nov 1915	The Nightbirds of London	*Hepworth*	(4)(P)

718 SINCLAIR, Upton Beall

May 1914	The Jungle	*All Star*	(5)(N)

719 SKINNER, Mrs Otis

Jul 1913	The Ne'er-to-return Road	*Selig*	(2)(S)

720 SMITH, Arden R.

Nov 1914	The Eagle's Nest *(see also* Arden*)*	*Lubin*	(5)(N)

721 SMITH, Edgar

Feb 1915	Old Dutch	*Shubert*	(5)(N)

722 SMITH, Francis Hopkinson

Sep 1912	Caleb West *(Caleb West, Master Driver)*	*Reliance*	(2)(S)
Apr 1913	Art and Honor *(An Old-Fashioned Gentleman)*	*Lubin*	(1)(S)
Apr 1913	Memories of His Youth *(An Old-Fashioned Gentleman)*	*Lubin*	(1)(S)
Jul 1915	Colonel Carter of Cartersville	*McIntosh*	(5)(S)

723 SMITH, Harry Bache

Mar 1914	The Billionaire	*Klaw & Erlanger*	(4)(P)

724 SMITH, Harry James

Sep 1915	Blackbirds	*Lasky*	(5)(N)

725 SMITH, Jesse Datus

Aug 1915	My Lost One	*Vitagraph*	(3)(S)

SMITH, Sarah *see* Stretton

726 SMITH, Winchell

Apr 1914	Brewster's Millions *(see also* McCutcheon; Stone*)*	*Lasky*	(5)(P)
Jun 1914	The Only Son	*Lasky*	(5)(P)
Aug 1914	The Fortune Hunter	*Lasky*	(6)(P)
Sep 1914	The Making of Bobby Burnit *(see also* Chester, George Randolph*)*	*Lasky*	(5)(P)
Sep 1915	Via Wireless *(see also* Armstrong*)*	*Pathé*	(5)(P)

727 SNYDER, John M.

Dec 1914	As Ye Sow	*Brady*	(5)(N)

728 SONNENBLICK, David

Mar 1915	From Headquarters	*Vitagraph*	(3)(S)

729 SOPHOCLES

1908	Oedipus Rex	*Film d'Art*	(1)(P)
May 1910	King Oedipus *(Oedipus Rex)*	*Cosmopolitan*	(1)(P)
1911	Antigone	*Cines*	(1)(P)
Dec 1912	Oedipus Rex	*Hecla*	(4)(P)

730 SOUSA, John Philip

Sep 1913	The Fifth String	*Selig*	(2)(S)

731 SOUTAR, Andrew

Jul 1915	A Bag of Gold	*Essanay*	(1)(S)

732 SOUVESTRE, Pierre

Oct 1909	The Two Burglars	*SCAGL*	(X)(S)
1913	Fantomas	*Gaumont*	(2)(N)

733 SPOONER, Cecil

Nov 1914	Nell of the Circus	*Sawyer*	(S)

734 STANTON, Coralie

Jul 1913	Zoe, A Woman's Last Card (*see also* Hosken)	*Hecla*	(3)(N)

735 STAPLETON, John

Mar 1915	A Gentleman of Leisure (*see also* Wodehouse)	*Lasky*	(5)(N)

STEARNS, Edgar Franklin *see* Franklin

736 STECK, H. Tipton

Aug 1914	Two Men Who Waited	*Essanay*	(1)(S)
Jan 1915	The Accounting	*Essanay*	(2)(S)
Mar 1915	The Great Silence	*Essanay*	(3)(S)

737 STEELE, Rufus

Mar 1915	Rule G. *(Keeping John Barleycorn off the Trains)*	*Blazon*	(2)(S)

738 STEGER, Julius

Mar 1915	The Fifth Commandment	*Cosmos*	(5)(N)
Dec 1915	The Warning	*Triumph*	(5)(N)

739 STEPHENSON, B. C.

Sep 1915	The Fatal Card (*see also* Chambers)	*Famous Players*	(5)(P)

740 STERNE, Elaine

Apr 1914	The Fruit of Evil *(Sins of the Father)*	*Nestor*	(2)(S)
Dec 1914	Without Hope	*Flamingo*	(4)(N)

741 STEVENS, John A.

May 1915	A Wife for a Wife	*Kalem*	(5)(N)

742 STEVENSON, Robert Louis

Feb 1908	Dr Jekyll and Mr Hyde	*Selig*	(1)(N)
Apr 1908	The Story of Treasure Island *(Treasure Island)*	*Vitagraph*	(1)(N)
Dec 1909	The Imp of the Bottle *(The Bottle Imp)*	*Edison*	(1)(S)
Jan 1910	A Modern Dr Jekyll and Mr Hyde *(Dr Jekyll and Mr Hyde)*	*Selig*	(X)(N)
Feb 1910	The Duality of Man *(Dr Jekyll and Mr Hyde)*	*Wrench*	(1)(N)
Jul 1910	Dr Jekyll and Mr Hyde	*Nordisk*	(1)(N)
Nov 1911	The Black Arrow	*Edison*	(1)(N)
Jan 1912	Dr Jekyll and Mr Hyde	*Thanhouser*	(1)(N)
May 1912	Treasure Island	*Edison*	(1)(N)
1912	Between Life and Death *(The Suicide Club)*	*Ambrosio*	(1)(S)
Mar 1913	Dr Jekyll and Mr Hyde	*Imp*	(2)(N)
1913	Dr Jekyll and Mr Hyde	*Kinemacolor*	(2)(N)
Nov 1913	Treasure Island	*Ranous*	(3)(N)
Dec 1913	A Modern Jekyll and Hyde *(Dr Jekyll and Mr Hyde)*	*Kalem*	(2)(N)
Jul 1914	The Suicide Club	*B&C*	(3)(S)
Jul 1914	Ebb-Tide	*Selig*	(3)(N)
Aug 1915	Horrible Hyde *(Dr Jekyll and Mr Hyde)*	*Lubin*	(2)(N)

743 STOCKTON, Frank R. (Francis Richard Stockton)

Nov 1908	The Lady or the Tiger?	*Edison*	(1)(S)

744 STONE, Melville

Apr 1914	Brewster's Millions (*see also* McCutcheon; Smith, Winchell)	*Lasky*	(5)(P)

745 STOREY, Fred

Mar 1914	Rip Van Winkle (*see also* Boucicault; Irving)	*Climax*	(3)(P)

746 STOWE, Harriet Elizabeth Beecher

May 1903	Uncle Tom's Cabin	*Lubin*	(X)(N)
Jul 1903	Uncle Tom's Cabin	*Edison*	(X)(N)
Nov 1905	The Barnstormers *(Uncle Tom's Cabin)*	*Biograph*	(X)(N)
Jul 1910	Uncle Tom's Cabin	*Thanhouser*	(1)(N)
Aug 1910	Uncle Tom's Cabin	*Vitagraph*	(3)(N)
Apr 1913	Uncle Tom's Cabin	*Imp*	(2)(N)
Apr 1913	An Uncle Tom's Cabin Troupe *(Uncle Tom's Cabin)*	*Biograph*	(1)(N)
Dec 1913	Uncle Tom's Cabin	*Kalem*	(20)(N)
Aug 1914	Uncle Tom's Cabin	*World*	(5)(N)

747 STRAUS, Oscar

Feb 1908	A Waltz Dream	*Duskes*	(X)(O)
Nov 1914	The Chocolate Soldier *(see also* Shaw*)*	*Whitney*	(4)(O)

748 STRAUSS, Richard

Apr 1910	Elektra	*Vitagraph*	(1)(O)

749 STREET, Julian Leonard

Jul 1915	Victorine *(The Goings-on of Victorine)*	*Majestic*	(2)(S)

750 STRETTON, Hesba (Sarah Smith)

Nov 1908	Jennifer's First Prayer *(Jessica's First Prayer)*	*Walturdaw*	(X)(N)

751 STRINGER, Arthur

Dec 1913	The Case of Cherry Purcell	*Edison*	(3)(S)
Dec 1915	The Secret Agent	*Rialto*	(5)(N)

752 STRONG, Austin

Mar 1914	A Good Little Devil	*Famous Players*	(5)(P)
	(see also Gerard; Rostand, Maurice*)*		

753 SUE, Eugène (Marie-Joseph Sue)

1909	The Mysteries of Paris	*Éclair*	(1)(N)
Mar 1913	The Wandering Jew	*Roma*	(4)(N)
May 1913	The Mysteries of Paris	*SCAGL*	(5)(N)
Apr 1913	Mathilde	*Éclair*	(2)(N)

754 SULLIVAN, Sir Arthur Seymour

May 1907	The Mikado	*Gaumont*	(X)(O)
	(see also Gilbert*)*		
Jul 1907	The Mikado	*Walturdaw*	(X)(O)
	(see also Gilbert*)*		
Aug 1907	The Yeomen of the Guard	*Walturden*	(X)(O)
	(see also Gilbert*)*		
Jun 1912	The Holy City	*Éclair*	(1)(Sg)

755 SUTRO, Alfred

Dec 1914	The Walls of Jericho	*Box Office*	(5)(P)
May 1915	The Builder of Bridges	*Frohman*	(5)(P)
Oct 1915	John Glayde's Honour	*Frohman*	(5)(P)

SUTTNER *see* von Suttner

756 SUZANNE, Gabrielle

Dec 1905	Beauty and the Beast	*Clarendon*	(1)(S)
Jun 1908	Beauty and the Beast	*Pathé*	(1)(S)
	(see also De Beaumont*)*		
Jun 1913	Beauty and the Beast	*Rex*	(2)(S)

757 SWIFT, Jonathan

Dec 1902	Gulliver's Travels	*Méliès*	(X)(N)
Apr 1903	Gulliver's Travels	*Lubin*	(X)(N)

758 SYKES, Percival H. T.

Aug 1904	An Affair of Honour	*Gaumont*	(X)(Pm)
May 1910	A Child's Message to Heaven	*Precision*	(1)(Pm)

759 TALBOT, Hayden

Dec 1914	The Truth Waggon	*Masterpiece*	(5)(N)

760 TANNER, James T.

Oct 1896	The Broken Melody (*see also* Keene)	*Collings*	(X)(P)
May 1909	A Gaiety Duet (*Our Miss Gibbs*)	*Gaumont*	(X)(P)

761 TARKINGTON, (Newton) Booth

Nov 1905	Monsieur Beaucaire	*Vitagraph*	(X)(N)
Feb 1913	Beau Brummell	*Vitagraph*	(1)(N)
Feb 1914	Sophia's Imaginary Visitors (*Beasley's Xmas Party*)	*Edison*	(1)(S)
Apr 1914	Cherry	*Vitagraph*	(1)(S)
May 1914	The Two Van Revels	*Edison*	(2)(S)
Nov 1914	The Man from Home (*see also* Wilson, Harry Leon)	*Lasky*	(4)(N)
Dec 1914	Springtime	*Life Photo*	(5)(N)
Dec 1914	Cameo Kirby (*see also* Wilson, Harry Leon)	*Lasky*	(5)(N)
Nov 1915	The Gentleman from Indiana	*Pallas*	(5)(N)
Dec 1915	Turmoil	*Columbia*	(5)(N)

762 TASSO, Torquato

Mar 1911	The Crusaders *(Jerusalem Delivered)*	*Cines*	(1)(Pm)

763 TAYLOR, Mary Imlay

Jul 1912	The Little Bride of Heaven	*Edison*	(1)(S)
May 1913	The Tenderfoot's Money	*Biograph*	(1)(S)
Mar 1914	The Impersonator	*Edison*	(3)(S)
Jun 1914	The Man in the Street	*Edison*	(2)(S)
Oct 1914	The Long Way	*Edison*	(3)(S)
Oct 1914	A Question of Identity *(The Window That Monsieur Forgot)*	*Edison*	(2)(S)
Jan 1915	The Magnate of Paradise	*Edison*	(2)(S)
Mar 1915	In the Shadow of Death *(Fate and the Pomegranates)*	*Edison*	(2)(S)
Oct 1915	Friend Wilson's Daughter	*Edison*	(3)(S)
Oct 1915	The Ploughshare	*Edison*	(4)(S)
Oct 1915	An Unwilling Thief	*Edison*	(4)(S)

TAYLOR, Hobart Chatfield *see* Chatfield-Taylor

764 TAYLOR, Tom

Aug 1912	Peg Woffington *(Masks and Faces)(see also* Reade*)*	*Britannia*	(2)(P)
May 1914	Clancarty	*London*	(2)(N)
Nov 1914	The Ticket-of-Leave Man	*Biograph*	(4)(P)

765 TENNYSON, Alfred, Lord

Apr 1908	Dora	*Vitagraph*	(1)(Pm)
Oct 1908	After Many Years *(Enoch Arden)*	*Biograph*	(1)(Pm)
Feb 1909	Forgotten *(Enoch Arden)*	*Eclipse*	(1)(Pm)
Nov 1909	Lancelot and Elaine *(Idylls of the King)*	*Vitagraph*	(1)(Pm)

Nov 1909	Dora	*Kalem*	(1)(Pm)
Dec 1910	Maud	*Clarendon*	(1)(Pm)
Dec 1910	The Golden Supper *(The Lover's Tale)*	*Biograph*	(1)(Pm)
May 1911	Lady Clare *(Lady Clare)*	*Thanhouser*	(1)(Pm)
Jul 1910	Becket	*Vitagraph*	(1)(P)
Jun 1911	Enoch Arden	*Biograph*	(2)(Pm)
Oct 1910	Dora	*Hepworth*	(X)(Pm)
Oct 1911	Lady Godiva *(Godiva)*	*Vitagraph*	(1)(Pm)
Jul 1912	Dora	*Powers*	(1)(Pm)
Sep 1912	The Charge of the Light Brigade	*Edison*	(1)(Pm)
Oct 1912	The Lady of Shalott	*Close*	(X)(Pm)
Oct 1912	Dora	*Biograph*	(1)(Pm)
Dec 1912	Lady Clare *(Lady Clare)*	*Edison*	(X)(Pm)
Jan 1913	A Day That Is Dead *(Break, Break, Break)*	*Edison*	(1)(Pm)
Jun 1913	Dora	*Majestic*	(1)(Pm)
Feb 1914	A Day That Is Gone *(Break, Break, Break)*	*Majestic*	(2)(Pm)
Sep 1914	The Charge of the Light Brigade	*Williams*	(1)(Pm)
Sep 1914	Break, Break, Break	*American*	(1)(Pm)
Nov 1914	Enoch Arden	*Neptune*	(3)(Pm)
Dec 1914	The Gardener's Daughter	*Clarendon*	(1)(Pm)
Mar 1915	Enoch Arden	*Majestic*	(4)(Pm)
Mar 1915	The Lady of Shalott	*Vitagraph*	(1)(Pm)
Aug 1915	Dora	*Biograph*	(3)(Pm)

766 TERHUNE, Albert Payson

Dec 1915	A Thief in the Night	*Lubin*	(2)(S)
Feb 1915	An Amateur Prodigal	*Essanay*	(2)(S)

767 TERRISS, William

Oct 1915	The Pearl of the Antilles *(The Sword of Honor)*	*Playhouse*	(5)(P)

768 THACKERAY, William Makepeace

Dec 1911	George Warrington's Escape *(The Virginians)*	*Selig*	(1)(N)
Dec 1911	Vanity Fair	*Vitagraph*	(3)(N)
Sep 1915	Vanity Fair	*Edison*	(7)(N)

THIBAULT, Jacques Anatole François *see* France

769 THOMAS, Ambroise (*see also* Goethe)

Dec 1909	A Bohemian Girl *(Mignon)*	*Cines*	(1)(P)
Jan 1912	Mignon or the Child of Fate	*Solax*	(1)(P)
Jan 1915	Mignon	*California*	(5)(P)

770 THOMAS, Augustus

Jul 1908	The Kentuckian	*Biograph*	(X)(P)
Aug 1913	Arizona	*All Star*	(5)(P)
Mar 1914	In Mizzoura	*All Star*	(5)(P)
Jun 1914	Soldiers of Fortune *(see also* Davis, Richard Harding*)*	*All Star*	(5)(P)
Nov 1914	The Education of Mr Pipp *(see also* Gibson*)*	*All Star*	(5)(P)
Jul 1915	Chimmie Fadden	*Famous Players*	(5)(P)
Jul 1915	The Earl of Pawtucket	*Universal*	(5)(P)
Oct 1915	Colorado	*Universal*	(5)(P)
Dec 1915	The Other Girl	*Raver*	(5)(P)

771 THOMAS, Brandon

Apr 1911	Charley's Aunt	*Monopol*	(1)(P)

772 THOMPSON, Charles M.

Jul 1914	The Painted Lady *(The Cavalier)*	*Majestic*	(2)(S)

Dec 1914	The Calico Cat	*Edison*	(2)(S)

773 THOMPSON, Denman

Nov 1915	Our New Minister	*Kalem*	(3)(Pm)
Dec 1915	The Old Homestead	*Famous Players*	(5)(Pm)

THOMPSON, Lillian Bennett *see* Bennett-Thompson

774 THORPE, Rose H.

Dec 1906	Curfew Shall Not Ring Tonight	*Gaumont*	(X)(Pm)
Jun 1909	The Curfew Bell *(Curfew Shall Not Ring Tonight)*	*Edison*	(1)(Pm)
May 1912	Curfew Shall Not Ring Tonight	*Reliance*	(1)(Pm)
Aug 1912	Curfew Shall Not Ring Tonight	*Hepworth*	(1)(Pm)
Nov 1913	Curfew Shall Not Ring Tonight	*Thanhouser*	(1)(Pm)

775 THURSTON, Ernest Temple

May 1914	Always Tell Your Wife	*Zenith*	(2)(P)
Nov 1915	Traffic	*Davidson*	(3)(N)

776 THURSTON, Katherine Cecil

Dec 1912	The Compact	*Pathé*	(1)(S)

777 TOLSTOI, Count Lev Nikolayevich

May 1909	Resurrection	*Biograph*	(1)(N)
Jul 1909	Resurrection	*Pathé*	(1)(N)
Dec 1910	Anna Karenina	*Pathé*	(X)(N)
1911	Anna Karenina	*SCAGL*	(1)(N)
1911	Resurrection	*Film d'Art*	(1)(N)
Jun 1912	Resurrection	*Masko*	(3)(N)
Oct 1912	Where Love Is, God Is Also	*Selig*	(1)(S)
Apr 1913	God Is Love	*Pathé*	(2)(S)

	(Where Love Is, God Is Also)		
Jul 1913	The Living Corpse	*Savoia*	(4)(N)
Mar 1915	The Kreutzer Sonata	*Fox*	(4)(S)
	(see also Gordin)		
Apr 1915	Anna Karenina	*Fox*	(5)(N)
May 1915	The Light of Truth	*Pathé*	(5)(N)

778 TOTTEN, Edith

Dec 1914	A Factory Magdalen	*Sawyer*	(5)(N)

779 TOWNSEND, Edward W.

Sep 1909	Little Sister	*Edison*	(X)(S)
Nov 1909	A Rose of the Tenderloin	*Edison*	(1)(S)
Mar 1910	A Victim of Bridge	*Edison*	(1)(S)
May 1910	Carmirella	*Edison*	(1)(S)
Jun 1910	The Piece of Lace	*Edison*	(1)(S)
Jun 1915	Chimmie Fadden	*Lasky*	(5)(P)
Nov 1915	Chimmie Fadden Out West	*Lasky*	(5)(P)

780 TRACY, Louis

Jul 1914	One Wonderful Night	*Essanay*	(4)(N)
	(see also Vance)		

781 TRAIN, Elizabeth Phipps

Apr 1914	A Social Highwayman	*Playgoers*	(4)(P)

782 TRANT, Joseph H.

May 1915	Princess Romanoff	*Fox*	(6)(N)
	(see also Sardou)		
Jun 1915	The Devil's Daughter	*Fox*	(5)(N)
	(see also D'Annunzio)		
Dec 1915	Juror Number Seven	*Rex*	(2)(S)

783 TRENCH, Herbert

May 1913	The Poet and the Soldier *(Apollo and the Seaman) (see also* French*)*	*Kalem*	(1)(Pm)

784 TREVOR, Leo

Feb 1915	Brother Officers	*London*	(4)(P)

785 TROWBRIDGE, John Townsend

Dec 1914	The Old Maid *(Dorothy in the Garret)*	*Majestic*	(2)(S)
Aug 1915	The Vagabonds *(Roger and I)*	*Thanhouser*	(2)(S)

786 TROWBRIDGE, W. H. R.

Nov 1915	The White Hope	*Hepworth*	(4)(N)

787 TRUMBULL, Annie Eliot

Oct 1912	A Christmas Accident	*Edison*	(1)(S)

788 TULLY, Richard Walton

Nov 1914	Rose of the Rancho *(see also* Belasco*)*	*Lasky*	(5)(P)

789 TURNBULL, Hector

Aug 1915	Out of the Darkness	*Lasky*	(5)(N)
Dec 1915	Temptation	*Lasky*	(5)(N)
Dec 1915	The Cheat	*Lasky*	(5)(N)

790 TURNBULL, Margaret

May 1914	Classmates *(see also* De Mille, William Churchill*)*	*Klaw & Erlanger*	(4)(P)

May 1915	Stolen Goods	*Lasky*	(5)(P)
Jul 1915	The Clue	*Lasky*	(5)(P)
Oct 1915	Secret Sin	*Lasky*	(5)(P)

TUTTIETT, Mary Gleed *see* Gray, Maxwell

791 TWAIN, Mark (Samuel Langhorne Clemens)

Mar 1907	A Curious Dream	*Vitagraph*	(X)(S)
Dec 1908	The Dancer and the King	*Vitagraph*	(X)(S)
Aug 1909	The Prince and the Pauper	*Edison*	(1)(N)
Mar 1910	A Mountain Blizzard *(Roughing It)*	*Edison*	(1)(bio)
Jul 1911	Science *(A Dog's Tale)*	*Imp*	(1)(S)
Dec 1914	The Dancer and the King	*World*	(5)(S)
Nov 1915	The Prince and the Pauper	*Famous Players*	(5)(N)

792 TYLER, Charles W.

Sep 1915	Across the Great Divide *(With Clear Rights)*	*Edison*	(1)(S)

UNSELL, Eve *see* Geoffreys

793 VACHELL, Horace Annesley

Oct 1915	Jelfs	*London*	(5)(P)

794 VALE, Travers

Oct 1913	The Girl of the Sunny South	*Kineto*	(4)(P)

795 VAN BUREN, Evelyn

Oct 1914	Left in the Train	*Thanhouser*	(1)(S)

796 VANCE, Louis Joseph

Jan 1914	The Day of Days	*Famous Players*	(4)(S)
Mar 1914	The Brass Bowl	*Edison*	(2)(S)
Jul 1914	One Wonderful Night *(See also* Tracy*)*	*Essanay*	(4)(S)
Jul 1914	The Trey O'Hearts	*Universal*	(Serial) (S)
Aug 1914	Sheep's Clothing	*Edison*	(2)(S)
Oct 1914	Terence O'Rourke, Gentleman Adventurer	*Universal*	(serial) (S)
Nov 1914	The New Adventures of Terence O'Rourke	*Universal*	(serial) (S)
Nov 1914	His Heart, His Hand and His Sword	*Victor*	(2)(S)
Mar 1915	The Spanish Jade *(see also* Hewlett*)*	*Fiction*	(5)(N)
Dec 1915	The Destroying Angel	*Edison*	(5)(N)

797 VANE, Sutton

Dec 1914	The Span of Life	*Kinephote*	(5)(P)
Aug 1915	The Cotton King	*Brady*	(5)(P)

798 VAN LOAN, Charles Emmett

Nov 1913	A Good Sport *(The International Cup)*	*Edison*	(2)(S)
Feb 1915	Buckshot John *(The Message to Buckshot John)*	*Bosworth*	(5)(N)
May 1915	Little Sunset	*Bosworth*	(5)(N)
Sep 1915	Buck Parvin	*Mustang*	(2)(S)
Oct 1915	Buck's Lady Friend	*Mustang*	(2)(S)
Oct 1915	A Man Afraid of His Wardrobe	*Mustang*	(3)(S)
Nov 1915	This is the Life	*Mustang*	(3)(S)
Dec 1915	Author, Author	*Mustang*	(3)(S)

799 VAN VORST, Marie

Jul 1915	The Girl from His Town	*American*	(5)(N)

800 VEILLER, Bayard

May 1915	The Fight	*World*	(5)(N)
Nov 1915	The Primrose Path	*Universal*	(5)(N)

801 VERDI, Giuseppe

Feb 1909	Il Trovatore	*Lubin*	(1)(O)
Feb 1909	A Fool's Revenge *(Rigoletto)(see also* Hugo*)*	*Biograph*	(1)(O)
Jun 1909	The Duke's Jester *(Rigoletto)(see also* Hugo*)*	*Vitagraph*	(1)(O)
Jun 1909	Rigoletto	*Film d'Art*	(1)(O)
Apr 1910	The Troubadour *(Il Trovatore)*	*Film d'Art*	(1)(O)
Jul 1910	Il Trovatore	*Animatophone*	(1)(O)
May 1911	Aida	*Edison*	(1)(O)
1911	Falstaff	*SCAGL*	(1)(O)
Dec 1913	Giuseppe Verdi: His Life and Glory	*Labor*	(5)(Biog)
Aug 1914	Il Trovatore	*Centaur*	(6)(O)

802 VERNE, Jules

Apr 1908	Michael Strogoff	*Essanay*	(1)(N)
Apr 1905	20,000 Leagues Under the Sea	*Biograph*	(1)(N)
Apr 1910	Michael Strogoff	*Edison*	(1)(N)
Nov 1913	20,000 Leagues Under the Sea	*Éclair*	(6)(N)
Apr 1914	In Search of the Castaways	*Éclair*	(5)(N)
May 1914	Michael Strogoff	*Popular*	(5)(N)
Jun 1914	Around the World in Eighty Days	*Pennant*	(6)(N)

803 VOLLMOELLER, Karl

Apr 1914	A Venetian Night	*Masko*	(4)(P)

1912	The Miracle	*Menschen*	(4)(P)

804 VON FLOTOW, Friedrich

Feb 1909	Duet for Marika *(Marika)*	*Lubin*	(X)(S)

805 VON MOSENTHAL, S. Herman Ritter (*see also* Daly)

Oct 1908	Leah the Forsaken *(Deborah)*	*Vitagraph*	(1)(P)
Sep 1912	Leah the Forsaken *(Deborah)*	*Imp*	(2)(P)

806 VON SUTTNER, Baroness Bertha Felice Sophie

Aug 1914	Lay Down Your Arms *(Ground Arms)*	*Nordisk*	(5)(N)

WADE, Rosalind Herschell *see* Carr, Catherine

807 WAGNER, Richard

Oct 1904	Parsifal	*Edison*	(X)(O)
Dec 1907	Parsifal	*Edison*	(2)(O)
Apr 1910	The Nibelungs *(Siegfried)*	*Cosmopolitan*	(X)(O)
Jun 1912	Siegfried	*Ambrosio*	(3)(O)
Nov 1912	Parsifal	*Ambrosio*	(3)(O)
Jul 1913	Tannhäuser	*Thanhouser*	(2)(O)

808 WALES, Hubert

Dec 1915	The Yoke	*YCC*	(4)(N)

809 WALES, Robert Ellis

Dec 1915	The Penitents	*Fine Arts*	(5)(N)

810 WALLACE, Lew(is)

Nov 1907	Ben Hur	*Kalem*	(1)(N)
Oct 1914	A Prince of India *(The Prince of India)*	*Eclectic*	(5)(N)

811 WALLERTON, Miles

May 1915	Another Man's Child	*B & C*	(4)(N)

812 WALTER, Eugene

Mar 1914	Paid in Full	*All Star*	(5)(N)
Jun 1914	The Wolf	*Lubin*	(5)(N)
Aug 1914	The Trail of the Lonesome Pine *(see also* Fox*)*	*Broadway*	(5)(N)
Jun 1915	Fine Feathers	*World*	(5)(N)

813 WATSON, Henry Brereton Marriott

Oct 1911	A Conspiracy Against the King *(The Cockerel)*	*Edison*	(1)(S)
Mar 1912	The Baby	*Edison*	(1)(S)
Mar 1912	Her Face	*Edison*	(1)(S)
Jan 1913	The Eldorado Lode	*Edison*	(1)(S)
Dec 1913	Stanton's Last Fling *(The Interlude)*	*Edison*	(1)(S)
Sep 1914	On the Isle of Sarne *(The Picaroon)*	*Edison*	(2)(S)

WAYNE, Charles Stokes *see* Hazeltine

814 WEATHERLEY, Frederick E.

Aug 1912	The Surgeon's Child	*Williams*	(1)(Pm)

815 WEBSTER, Henry Kitchell

May 1915	The Butterfly	*Shubert*	(5)(P)
Oct 1915	Comrade John *(see also* Merwin*)*	*Balboa*	(5)(N)
Nov 1915	The Green Cloak	*Kleine*	(5)(N)

816 WEBSTER, Merwin

Sep 1912	Calumet K	*Edison*	(1)(S)

817 WELLS, Carolyn

Oct 1909	The Three Kisses	*Edison*	(X)(S)
1909	The Wallace Jewels	*Edison*	(1)(S)
1910	History Repeats Itself	*Edison*	(1)(S)
Sep 1911	That Winsome Winnie Smile	*Edison*	(1)(S)
Apr 1912	Winnie's Dance	*Edison*	(1)(S)
Jul 1913	Winsome Winnie's Way	*Edison*	(1)(S)
Aug 1913	The Mystery of West Sedgewick *(The Gold Bag)*	*Edison*	(2)(S)

818 WESTCOTT, Edward Noyes

Feb 1915	David Harum	*Famous Players*	(5)(N)

819 WESTERVELT, Leonidas

Dec 1915	The Siren's Song *(see also* Middleton*)*	*Shubert*	(5)(P)

820 WEYMAN, Stanley John

Oct 1915	Under the Red Robe *(see also* Rose*)*	*Clarendon*	(4)(N)

821 WHALEN, William H.

Jul 1915	Ill-Starred Barbie	*Balboa*	(5)(N)

822 WHEELER, A. C.

Mar 1914	The Great Diamond Robbery	*Playgoers*	(6)(P)
	(see also Alfriend*)*		

823 WHITE, Grace Miller

Mar 1914	Tess of the Storm Country	*Famous Players*	(4)(N)
Mar 1915	From the Valley of the Missing	*Fox*	(5)(N)
May 1915	The Plunderer	*Fox*	(5)(N)
	(see also Norton*)*		

824 WHITE, John

Dec 1915	Wild Oats	*Kleine*	(5)(N)
	(see also Gollan*)*		

825 WHITE, Stewart Edward

Aug 1914	The Call of the North	*Lasky*	(5)(N)
	(Conjurer's House)(see also Broadhurst*)*		
May 1913	Ashes of Three	*American*	(2)(S)
Jun 1913	A Garden Party in California	*American*	(X)(S)

826 WHITTIER, John Greenleaf

Oct 1908	Barbara Frietchie	*Vitagraph*	(X)(Pm)
Feb 1909	Mogg Megone	*Vitagraph*	(X)(Pm)
Oct 1909	Maud Muller	*Essanay*	(1)(Pm)
Oct 1911	Maud Muller	*Selig*	(1)(Pm)
Aug 1912	Maud Muller	*Nestor*	(2)(Pm)
Mar 1915	The Bay of Seven Isles	*Laemmle*	(2)(Pm)
Nov 1915	Barbara Frietchie	*Popular*	(5)(Pm)
	(see also Fitch, Clyde*)*		

WIENER, Frantz *see* De Croisset

827 WILCOX, Ella Wheeler

Feb 1913	The Two Glasses	*Pilot*	(1)(Pm)
Dec 1914	The Price He Paid	*Humanology*	(1)(Pm)
1915	Lord, Speak Again	*Humanology*	(1)(Pm)

828 WILDE, Oscar (Fingall O'Flahertie Wills)

Aug 1908	Salome	*Vitagraph*	(X)(P)
1908	Salome	*SCAGL*	(1)(P)
Oct 1910	Dorian Gray's Portrait *(The Picture of Dorian Gray)*	*Regia*	(1)(N)
1913	The Picture of Dorian Gray	*Skandinavisk*	(2)(N)
1913	Dorian Gray *(The Picture of Dorian Gray)*	*New York*	(2)(N)
Nov 1913	A Florentine Tragedy	*Warner*	(3)(S)
Jul 1915	The Picture of Dorian Gray	*Thanhouser*	(2)(N)

829 WILKES, W. E.

1913	Broken Threads	*Kaybee*	(2)(S)

830 WILLIAMS, Bransby

Jun 1914	Bernardo's Confession	*Planet*	(1)(P)
Jun 1914	The Street Watchman's Story	*Planet*	(1)(P)

831 WILLIAMS, Percival

Jan 1915	The Italian	*Domino*	(2)(S)
1915	The Alibi *(The Sign of the Rose)*	*Kay Bee*	(2)(S)

832 WILLIAMS, Thomas J.

Mar 1913	Turn Him Out	*Selig*	(2)(S)

833 WILLIAMSON, Mrs C. N.

Jun 1915	The House of the Lost Court	*Edison*	(5)(N)

Dec 1915	Lord John's Journal	*Universal*	(serial) (N)

834 WILLIS, F. McGrew

Nov 1915	Under a Shadow *(A Secret Service Affair)*	*Rex*	(2)(S)

835 WILLS, W. G.

Mar 1915	Jane Shore *(see also* Rowe*)*	*Barker*	(6)(P)

836 WILSON, Augusta Jane Evans

Mar 1910	St. Elmo	*Thanhouser*	(1)(N)
Apr 1910	St. Elmo	*Vitagraph*	(1)(N)
May 1914	St. Elmo	*Balboa*	(6)(N)
Apr 1915	Beulah	*Balboa*	(6)(N)
Jun 1915	God's Witness *(At the Mercy of Tiberius)*	*Thanhouser*	(5)(N)
Sep 1915	Infelice	*Samuelson*	(6)(N)

837 WILSON, Francis

Jan 1915	The Butterfly on the Wheel	*Box Office*	(5)(N)

838 WILSON, Harry Leon (*see also* Tarkington)

Nov 1914	The Man from Home	*Lasky*	(5)(N)
Dec 1914	Cameo Kirby	*Lasky*	(5)(N)

839 WINSPEARE, Arthur

Feb 1910	A Noble Sacrifice	*Novone*	(1)(S)

840 WINTER, John Strange (Henrietta Eliza Vaughan Palmer)

Jun 1911	Bootle's Baby	*Edison*	(1)(N)
Aug 1914	Bootle's Baby	*London*	(4)(N)
Oct 1914	Bootle's Baby	*Edison*	(5)(N)
Oct 1914	Beautiful Jim	*B & C*	(3)(N)
Jul 1915	Grip	*B & C*	(3)(N)
Aug 1915	Lady Jennifer	*YCC*	(4)(N)

841 WISE, Thomas Alfred

Oct 1914	The Gentleman from Mississippi (*see also* Rhodes, Harrison Garfield)	*Brady*	(5)(N)

842 WISEMAN, Cardinal Nicholas Patrick Stephen

Dec 1910	The Sword and the Cross (*Fabiola*)	*Gaumont*	(1)(N)

843 WISTER, Owen

Mar 1910	A Western Romance (*The Westerner*)	*Edison*	(X)(N)
Sep 1914	The Virginian (*see also* La Shelle)	*Lasky*	(5)(N)

844 WODEHOUSE, Sir Pelham Grenville

Mar 1915	A Gentleman of Leisure (*see also* Stapleton)	*Lasky*	(5)(N)
Aug 1915	Rule 63	*Essanay*	(2)(S)

845 WOLF, Rennold

Jun 1915	My Best Girl (*see also* Pollock)	*Rolfe*	(5)(N)

846 WONDERLY, William Carey

Aug 1914	The Second Mrs Roebuck *(The Smart Set)*	*Majestic*	(2)(N)
Feb 1915	The Lost Lord Lovell	*Majestic*	(2)(N)

847 WOOD, Mrs Henry (Ellen Price)

Sep 1902	East Lynne	*Harrison*	(X)(N)
Jun 1908	East Lynne	*Vitagraph*	(X)(N)
Jun 1908	East Lynne	*Selig*	(X)(N)
Jul 1909	Led Astray *(East Lynne)*	*Vitagraph*	(X)(N)
Oct 1910	East Lynne	*Precision*	(1)(N)
Jan 1912	East Lynne	*Thanhouser*	(1)(N)
May 1913	East Lynne	*Barker*	(6)(N)
Jun 1913	East Lynne	*Brightonia*	(2)(N)
Sep 1914	East Lynne in Bugville *(East Lynne)*	*Crystal*	(1)(N)
Jul 1915	East Lynne	*Biograph*	(3)(N)

848 WOODROW, Mrs Wilson (Nancy Mann)

Nov 1914	Olive's Opportunities	*Edison*	(serial)(S)
Dec 1914	The Battle of Love	*Essanay*	(3)(N)
Jun 1915	The Tragedies of the Crystal Globe	*Edison*	(3)(S)

849 WOODRUFF, Helen S.

Apr 1915	The Lady of the Lighthouse	*Vitagraph*	(5)(N)

850 WOODRUFF, Henry

Dec 1911	Brown of Harvard *(see also* Young, Rida Johnson*)*	*Selig*	(1)(N)

851 WORRALL, Letchmere

Jul 1915	The Man Who Stayed at Home *(see also* Grey*)*	*Hepworth*	(3)(P)

852 WYLIE, Ida Alexa Ross

Dec 1915	The Unknown *(The Red Mirage)*	*Lasky*	(5)(N)
Mar 1915	The Man in Motley	*Essanay*	(1)(S)

853 WYSS, Johann David and Johann Rudolf

May 1903	The Swiss Family Robinson	*Lubin*	(X)(N)

854 YATES, Edmund

May 1915	The Black Sheep	*Biograph*	(2)(N)

855 YONGE, Charlotte Mary

Jan 1913	The Dove in the Eagle's Nest	*Thanhouser*	(2)(N)

856 YOUNG, Sir Charles Lawrence

Jun 1915	Jim the Penman	*Famous Players*	(5)(P)

857 YOUNG, Rida Johnson

Dec 1911	Brown of Harvard *(see also* Woodruff, Henry*)*	*Selig*	(1)(P)

858 YOUNG, W.

Mar 1911	The Rajah	*Edison*	(1)(S)

859 ZAMLOCH, A. F.

Aug 1913	The Magician Fisherman	*Selig*	(1)(S)

860 ZANGWILL, Israel

Jan 1915	Children of the Ghetto	*Box Office*	(5)(N)

Apr 1915	The Melting Pot	*Cort*	(5)(P)

861 ZOLA, Émile

Mar 1909	Drink *(L'Assommoir)*	*SCAGL*	(1)(N)
Mar 1909	A Drunkard's Reformation *(L'Assommoir)*	*Biograph*	(X)(N)
1909	Faldgruben *(L'Assommoir)*	*Biorama*	(1)(N)
Aug 1910	The Attack on the Mill	*Edison*	(1)(S)
Apr 1911	Mennenskedyret	*Kinografen*	(1)(S)
May 1912	Nana	*Skandinavisk*	(2)(N)
1912	Au Pays de Ténèbres *(Germinal)*	*Éclair*	(2)(N)
Oct 1913	Germinal	*SCAGL*	(6)(N)

Title Index

This index lists every title in this catalogue, including original titles of works where they have been changed by the film producers. The numbers refer to the entry (author) numbers, not the page numbers. Initial articles (*a*, *an*, *the*, *il*, *la*, *le*, *les*, etc.) have been omitted here, but will be found in the main entries.

Appendix

Alphabetical list of film production companies by country

Britain

Animatographe
Arrow
B & C (British & Colonial)
Barker (William)
BEF (British Empire)
Brightonia
Britannia
Brittanic
Broadwest
Buckland (Warwick)
Walterdaw
Cinema Productions
Clarendon
Climax
Close (Ivy)
Collings (Esme)
Cooperative
Cricks (George)
Davidson
Gaumont
Gibbons (Walter)
H & W
Haggar (William)
Harrison
Hepworth (Cecil)
Heron
Holmfirth
Kearton (Cherry)
London
Lucrative
McEvoy (Charles)
Magnet
Martin
Mitchell & Kenyon
MLB
Neptune
Paul (Robert)
Planet
Precision
Regal
Renaissance
Riley Brothers
Ruffells
Samuelson (George)
Smith (George)
Sunny South
T & G (Theatre & General)
Terrier
Turner (Florence)
UK
Urban (Charles)
Walturdaw
Warwick
Williams (Eric)
Williamson (James)
YCC (Yorkshire Cine)
Zenith

France

Cosmopolitan
Éclair
Éclipse
Film d'Art
Gaumont
Lion
Lumière
Méliès (Georges)
Pathé
Raleigh & Robert
SCAGL

Germany

Biorama
Bioskop
Duskes
Kinografen
Leemund
Menschen

Thiemann
Vitaskop

Italy

Ambrosio
Aquila
Cines
Itala
Labor
Lux
Milano
Pasquali
Roma
Savoia

United States of America

Alco
Alhambra
All Star
Alliance
American
Art
Balboa
Beauty
Biograph
Bison
Blaché (Herbert)
Bosworth (Hobart)
Box Office
Brady (William)
Broadway
Broncho
California
Centaur
Challenge
Champion
Circle
Climax
Colonial
Columbia
Cort
Cosmo
Crescent
Crystal
Domino
Dormet
Dryeda
Eastern
Eclair
Eclectic
Edison (Thomas A.)
Epoch
Equitable
Essanay
Excelsior
Famous Players
Favorite
Feature
Fiction
Filmotions
Fine Arts
Flamingo
Fox (William)
Fraser
Frohman
Gardner (Helen)
Garrison
Gem
Gold Seal
Goodfellow
Great Players
Griffith (D. W.)
Humanology
Ince (Thomas)
Johnson
Juno
Kalem
Kaybee
Keedrick
Kennedy (Joseph)
Kinemacolor
Klaw & Erlanger
Kleine
Knickerbocker
Komic
Lasky (Jesse L.)
Leading Players
Leonard (Marion)
Liberty
Liebler
Life Photo
Loftus
Lubin (Sigmund)
McIntosh
Majestic
Masterpiece
Metro
Mirrorgraph
Mohawk
Monopol
Moore
Morosco (Oliver)
Motion Drama
Mustang
Mutual
National
Nestor
New York
Nonpareil
Novelty
Novone
Ocean
Oz

Paramount
Pallas
Pathé
Peerless
Pennant
Phoenix
Photodrama
Photoplay
Pilot
Playgoers
Playhouse
Popular
Powers (Pat)
Premier
Premo
Progressive
Prohibition
Puritan
Quality
Ramo
Ranous
Raver (Harry)
Reliable
Reliance
Rialto
Rolfe
Rosenberg
Sawyer
Select
Selig (William)
Shakespeare
Shubert
Solax
Standard
Sterling
Thanhouser
Triangle
Triumph
Union
Universal
Utah
Victor
Vitagraph
Warner
Wharton (Theodore)
Whitney
World

Others

Australia
Canadian Bioscope
Dania
Hecla
Helios
Masko
Nordisk
Ouki
Regia
Skandinavisk
Tait